UNITY OF GOD AND UNITY IN GOD

Mohammad Ali Shomali

Wings of Unity Series, Part One:

UNITY OF GOD AND UNITY IN GOD

Mohammad Ali Shomali

ISBN: 978-1-904934-25-7

Second Edition 2017 First published

in Great Britain in 2017

Reprinted in 2018

Institute of Islamic Studies

140 Maida Vale, London W9 1QB

Tel: (44) 0207 604 5500; Fax: (44) 0207 604 4898

Email: icel@ic-el.com

Table of Contents

Foreword..5

Unity of God and Unity in God 13

    Unity of God as one of the main principles of Islam........14

    Islamic Philosophy..21

    Notion of existence in the Transcendent Philosophy 21

    Notion of light in the Illuminationist Philosophy 23

    Everything is a sign of God 25

        The face of God 27

God's Plan for Humanity in Creation 43

God's Plan for Humanity in Guidance..................59

    The elements which help to unite religions 68

    I. Spirituality..68

    II. Knowledge 71

    III. Emotional growth..74

    IV. Attacks against religion 77

God's Plan for End of the Time 85

    Imam Mahdi and Jesus come together 87

    Some qualities of the companions of Imam Mahdi 88

    Lake and ocean of united drops................................89

    Human beings are like one body 90

    Circulation of blood in the body 91

In the Name of God, the Compassionate, the Merciful

Foreword

What we learn from the Qur'an is that whenever there is darkness there will also be light, wherever there is difficulty there will be ease too. We are currently living in a world with many tensions, conflicts and wars, but thanks be to God, in the same world we have lots of people who are deeply committed to love, peace and charity, especially from among the believers in God. There are people who tirelessly work for unity and peace. For quite a few years we have come to know such groups of people among both the Muslim and non-Muslim communities.

We have had long-standing relations with some Christian movements and groups and despite our theological differences we have realised how many commonalities we have, not only in our understanding of God and humanity, but in understanding the priorities for the religious work of today. These are people who believe there is urgency to work for the sake of unity.

It is almost twenty years since we have established a relationship with the Focolare Movement during which we had many meetings and constructive discussions. This connection started initially in the UK but soon it expanded to Italy, Canada, Indonesia, Lebanon, Poland, the Philippines, USA and many other places. Here I just refer to our visits to Loppiano in general and Sophia University Institute in particular.

Our first visit to Loppiano was in 1999, on the eve of the new millennium. In May 2010, I took a group of PhD students from the Dept. of Religions of the Imam Khomeini Education and Research Institute in Qom to Italy to visit some Pontifical universities and some Catholic institutions and organisations. A highlight of that trip was visiting Loppiano. An interesting development took place in May 2013 when my wife and I took a group of 10 female students from the Jami'at al-Zahra, made up of peoples from different nationalities, from Qom to Italy. Most of our programmes were arranged by the Focolare Movement. We had programmes and meetings in Rome, in Rocca di Pappa, in Castel Gandolfo and also Loppiano, a small village near Florence where the movement has a citadel known as a 'Mariapolis'. This is a place individuals attend for their own religious development. There are also families living there in a spiritual atmosphere of mutual cooperation and unity. On the last night of our trip we met the inhabitants of the town in a gathering held at the local auditorium and had a discussion centred on the concept of love. I personally experienced a great sense of unity as if our hearts where open to each other. I understand that the same was felt by many among those present.

In recent years the Focolare Movement have also established 'Sophia University' in Loppiano which offers post-graduate studies. After this meeting another turning point was the invitation of members of the Centre for Interreligious Dialogue of Focolare Movement: Roberto Catalano and then co-responsible Christina Lee, together with Paul Lemarie, a member of the centre as well as a member of the Focolar from Loppiano and finally Stefania Tanesini. They visited us in Qom in April 2014 for one week where they were introduced to cultural, religious and spiritual aspects of the life of Shi'a Muslims.

That visit led to another trip in 2015 by about half a dozen sisters from Qom to Loppiano, to observe in more detailed some aspects of Focolare spirituality. The group travelled from Qom and Dearborn and was supposed to stay for four weeks. My wife and I also joined them from London and were supposed to stay with the group for a few days and then return. However due to the loss of my wife's passport at the airport, our stay was extended unexpectedly which turned out to be most useful. On Friday 20th Feb 2015, our Focolare friends organised a programme at 'Sophia University' where we met staff and students. I was asked to say a few words and I decided to talk about 'wisdom' which in Greek is 'sophia' from which the university takes its name.

I explained the Islamic point of view on wisdom and how it is a universal value, as anything truly wise belongs to the whole of humanity. In my talk I also mentioned the founder of the Focolare Movement Chiara Lubich (1920-2008) and my opinion about her wisdom and her practical spirituality through which she was able, not only to bring spirituality to the ordinary people but to build concrete realities based on it. This is an expression of wisdom, because wisdom is to bring abstract ideas into reality.

In the same meeting, Professor Piero Coda, president of Sophia University, invited me to teach in a forthcoming course on interreligious dialogue. The course would – for the first time – feature lecturers from different religious backgrounds. He also invited me for a similar engagement in the Philippines.

In April 2016, I visited Sophia University and delivered four lectures of one hour each on interreligious dialogue from an Islamic prospective. At the end, in a meeting with Piero Coda, I emphasised the necessity of a closer relationship to achieve a better understanding of what true commitment to unity requires from us. I said that the issue of unity and in particular how to unite believers has preoccupied my mind for many years. I said that I believe that if we do our best, God would certainly guide us and teach us what to do next, but in order to make sure that we have done our best we need to share our resources and exchange our ideas;

otherwise we would not be able to say that we have gone through every possible avenue for better understanding. I said to him if I talk and discuss only with my own people using only my own resources I cannot say I have done my best and the same applies to him. I referred to what God says in the Qur'an:

"As for those who strive in Us, We shall surely guide them in Our ways, and God is indeed with the virtuous". (29:69).

Therefore I suggested further meetings every so often to allow us to have detailed conversations on common interests and hopefully by recording and documenting our understanding we may be able to see if there is further grounds to continue or not. But we have to be able to say we have done our best. Piero welcomed the idea and based on that we fixed the date for the first meeting to take place after the month of Ramadan. This was going to be a new and deeper initiative built upon our previous experiences. We agreed to call this new initiative 'Wings of Unity'.

Our first 'Wings of Unity' meeting took place in Loppiano from 8th-10th July. A group of Focolare professors, staff and students from different parts of Italy also attended but there were more attendees from Sophia University and the Loppiano community.. From the Shi'a side there were five of us, from the UK, the USA and Italy. Piero Coda opened the meeting on the morning of the 8thJuly talking about the 'Unity of God and in God'. He explained some of the

9

mystical writings and experiences of Chiara Lubich. He referred in particular to the love for God the Father and love for one's neighbours.

In the afternoon session I talked about the Unity of God and how in Islam tawhid (unity of God) shapes and forms every aspect of Islamic thought. I explained how over the years I have been thinking about the issue of unity to the extent that one could write a book on it and each chapter of this book can discuss one aspect of this unity. I started mentioning some titles for chapters of that book e.g. metaphysics and how in the 'Transcendent Philosophy' of Mulla Sadra we have a kind of monotheistic understanding of existence. I talked about 'Illuminationist Philosophy' of Sheikh Shahab al-Din Suhrawardi in his Hikmat ul-ishraq and his philosophical system, based on the concept of light. I talked about the Unity of God as the basis for morality in the Qur'an, as suggested by Allamah Tabatabai. This was followed by further discussions.

The next day started with a comment from one of the professors from Sophia University. He remarked that as a PhD professor he had been teaching interfaith dialogue for a number of years, but this new initiative was the first time that he felt the presence of so much unity. He said he always tried to understand the other or look at the other in a way that he himself wants to be seen but this gathering went further, as if there was no 'other'.

On the second day, Roberto Catalano gave a talk titled 'Humanity as one family in Chiara'. He explained how the Focolare Movement got involved in interreligious dialogue. Initially Chiara had thought that the Focolare spirituality was only for Catholics and then for the wider Christians but after some events she got the inspiration that this should be open to everybody. He mentioned how the movement got to know Warith Deen Mohammed, imam of the Nation of Islam and how she also visited Malik el-Shabazz (Malcolm X) Mosque in Harlem – New York. He further described her travel to India and her interaction with the Hindus showing a video of the trip. In the afternoon I talked about my understanding of the plan of God for human guidance and the relationship between different prophets and religions.

On the morning of the third day two professors from Focolare spoke about Unity as Lifestyle according to the Christian Focolare perspective. I also presented our perspective about Unity as a lifestyle using some of the analogies or parables that we have in Islam such as the community being like one body or one building. I explained how I can see some of the qualities in some of the practices of the Focolare Movement that should be present in the believers, especially the helpers of Imam Mahdi (a). For example, they act as members of the same family as if brought up by the same parents. My presentation was followed by further discussions after which some suggestions were made about our next steps.

Professor Piero Coda suggested we define the mission statement of the 'Wings of Unity' initiative therefore it was decided that there would be two co-directors, Prof. Piero Coda and I, coupled with a council made up of four Focolare members and four Shi'a Muslim members. God-willing, Wings of Unity will continue its discussions, joint courses and joint publications. There will be courses on theology and spirituality of unity for both Muslim and Christian youth, Imams, priests, monks and activists. A book will also be produced on unity, faith, identity etc. based on the questions which will be raised by the youths in the courses next summer.

In brief, I can say that this meeting and exchange in Loppiano was very special and a memorable experience. Everyone was deeply moved by this experience of unity and expressed a desire in its continuation. We thank God for this great gift of friendship and unity and request Him to help us to move forward.

What follows is the transcript of three lectures delivered on 8th to 10th July 2016 at Sophia Institute University in Loppiano, Italy. I hope the readers find this humble collection useful and share with me their comments.

Unity of God and Unity in God[1]

I seek assistance and guidance from God. At the beginning, I must admit that I am unable to do justice to the topic. I will just try to share with you some aspects of unity based on the Quran, on Islamic thought in general, and on some of my personal reflections. We will then see how the discussion will unfold.

Although unity of God for us is a very important principle in Islam but for me to think very seriously about the unity of God in a way that should affect our relation with each other is something that I have been thinking and reflecting more seriously about in the last eight years.

There are many, many resources in Islam for unity. Some of them may have not been noticed, even by Muslims. Or if they are noticed, they are noticed for other purposes and not so much from this perspective of uniting people. I was thinking for some time that when I get a chance, maybe I

---

[1] This lecture was delivered on the 8th July 2016.

will write a book on unity; it would have different chapters and each chapter would be on one Islamic notion that helps us better understand the concept of unity. It would have many chapters because there are many things in Islam on unity. I think this approach to unity can be a kind of philosophy for life. So this is one of my projects for unity. I don't know when I will get a chance to complete it.

I want to first share, very quickly, a list of some of these notions which can be some of the titles for those chapters. Then I will focus on two or three of them. But I think it is good to share a list of these topics, because you may find that one of these topics is actually more interesting to you and you might prefer I talk about that instead.

Unity of God as one of the main principles of Islam

First of all, as you know, Muslims believe in the unity of God. In Shi‘a Islam, we say that we have three principles of religion, which means that every religious person in the Abrahamic tradition believes in these. The three principles are as follows: to believe in one God (unity of God or monotheism), to believe in prophethood and to believe in resurrection. We Shi‘a have two more in addition to these three: divine justice – also reflected as social justice – and imamate, which is the need for divinely-appointed leadership. Therefore these are five principles for Shi‘a

Muslims. The first three are known as "principles of religion" (*usul al-din*) and the five together are known as "principles of the denomination" (*usul al-madhhab*).

When it comes to the unity of God, unfortunately, many people keep it only in the realm of theology. When I say theology I mean Islamic theology, because in Christianity theology embraces everything but in Islam theology is a very specific type of discourse, a discussion about God; a kind of theosophy. Not much emphasis has been put by some Muslim scholars to bring unity of God into different realms of Islamic thought, but some have done so.

When we refer to the sayings of the Prophet (s) and our Imams, we find that they believe that the unity of God is not only the core and foundation, but it is in a sense, the only thing that you need. For example, it is narrated that Prophet Muhammad (s) used to say:

> Say, there is no God but the One God, and
> then you will be triumphant.[2]

It seems that to begin with the Prophet did not give the people a list of 10 or 20 or 100 things. He just emphasized on one thing: unity of God. Of course, this does not mean

---

[2] *Bihār al-Anwār*, vol. 18, p. 202. The original text is as follows:

يَا أَيُّهَا النَّاسُ قُولُوا لا إِلَهَ إِلا اللَّهُ تُفْلِحُوا

that we do not have any other things to believe in but it means that if people accept this, all other good things will follow.

Sometimes I say to people that prophets have wisdom; if there are hundreds of problems in the society they know which problems are the most important and they focus on those problems. Prophet Muhammad (s), with the wisdom and guidance that he received from God, realized and was able to identify that in that society in which there were many problems and lots of corruption – killing, looting, idol-worshipping, even burying daughters alive – the major problem is lack of recognition for unity of God in both their thought and practice.

We have another narration (*hadith*) from our 8th Imam, Imam Rida (a) who is buried in Mashhad, Iran. He used to live in Medina and Ma'mun, the Abbasid caliph of the time, forced him to become his prince. He did not accept at first but was forced to accept the position, so he said I will accept under the condition that I don't deal with any governmental affairs, I don't appoint anyone, I don't dismiss anyone, I don't take any job. Because he was very popular so the caliph wanted to use his popularity. Then the caliph asked him to move to the city of Marw where the caliph himself resided.[3] When Imam was going to that area in the city of Neishabūr –

---

[3] Which is now in Afghanistan but at that time was still in Iran.

which is now about 130 km away from (the city of) Mashhad – he was stopped by thousands of people. Most of them were not Shi'a, but they loved him because he was from the progeny of the Prophet (s).

So they asked him for some advice, and he said something that came to be known as the Golden Chain Hadith. This is because he said, "I heard this from my father (the 7th Imam), and my father heard it from the 6th Imam… (finally) who heard it from the Prophet (s), the Prophet (s) heard it from Gabriel, and Gabriel heard it from God:

> The word (of unity) 'there is no god but Allah' is My fortress; whoever enters My fortress will be saved from My punishment.

It is echoing the same thing the Prophet (s) used to say, which means that you do not need anything else next to or added to the unity of God.

Then the Imam moved and stopped, after which he said, "But there are conditions for this, and I am one of the conditions."[4] It means to believe in a divinely-appointed position is a condition for being loyal or faithful to *tawhīd*

---

[4] *Amālī (Sadūq)*, p. 235. The original text is as follows:

لا إِلَهَ إِلا اللَّهُ حِصْنِى فَمَنْ دَخَلَ حِصْنِى أَمِنَ مِنْ عَذَابِى فَلَمَّا مَرَّتِ الرَّاحِلَةُ نَادَانَا بِشُرُوطِهَا وَ أَنَا مِنْ شُرُوطِهَا.

(unity of God). It is not something additional to *tawḥīd*. This is very, very important. We do not need to add anything to unity; rather, unity brings many, many other things. There are many, many conditions for being committed to unity, but you do not need to bring anything to unity. Unity has to remain one. It is not one of many, it is just one. Everything comes under that. In the same way that God is one, the principle of unity is also one; other things come under it.

So we find that if human beings fully understand the meaning of God's oneness then their lives totally change. But oftentimes, because we do not understand the meaning of the oneness of God, we take it just as a dogma in theology. I can believe in the oneness of God and still have lots of problems; I can be a person who believes in the oneness of God and be selfish or greedy. But if someone really, truly, sincerely believes in the oneness of God, they cannot suffer from selfishness, greediness, and so on and so forth. It is impossible.

One of our great contemporary scholars who is a philosopher, mystic, and exegete of the Quran, 'Allāhmah Tabātabā'ī has authored many books and one of them is a 20-volume commentary on the Quran entitled *Al-Mīzān fī Tafsīr al-Qur'an,* which we believe is the best until now. He makes a very important point about the relation between the unity of God and morality. He says that there have been different attitudes towards moral improvement. Some philosophers or religious people have tried to encourage people to be moral by highlighting the good or bad outcomes of our actions in this world. For example, "if you tell a lie it will have bad outcomes, and so you shouldn't tell lies in order to avoid these bad outcomes." Or "if you are honest, these are the good outcomes, so you should be honest." This is one approach. The other approach is to use reward and punishment: "if you do good God will reward you and if you do bad God will punish you." And he says that although the Quran uses both of these approaches, as far as he knows, the Quran has a unique, third approach, and that is to base morality "on pure and perfect monotheism."[5]

---

[5] *Al-Mizan fi Tafsir al-*Qur'an, verses 2:153-157. Allamah Tabataba'i explains further:

> There is a third system, which is found exclusively in the Qur'an; it is neither seen in the Divine Books which have been transmitted to us, nor in the teachings of the previous prophets (peace of Allah be on them!); nor is it seen in the knowledge which has come to us from divine scholars. In this system, man is trained in character and knowledge, and the knowledge is used in a way that does not leave room for base and low traits. In other words, this system removes the vile characteristics, not by repulsing them, but by eliminating all motives other than Allah.

He goes on saying:

> The Qur'an has repeatedly said that the kingdom belongs to Allah, that the kingdom of the heavens and the earth is His, that to Him belongs all that is in the heavens and the earth, as we have explained several times. Evidently, this kingdom does not leave any

If you are a real monotheist, then all vicious actions stop and all vicious qualities would be removed. How can a person really believe in God as the only source of good, as the only source of success, and then be jealous? If you really understand what it means to be a believer in one God, then you would not be jealous or would not be fearful or greedy. The reason we may have this problem is because we have not really committed ourselves to the truth and reality of the unity of God. We just talk about it or believe in it in our minds, but we do not live and practice the unity of God.

independence to anything, nor does it allow the creatures any freedom from want - except through Allah. Look at anything; you will see that Allah is the Owner of its person and of all its concomitants. When a man believes in that owner-ship and this belief becomes firmly-rooted in his heart, he does not admit that anything has got any independence at all - in its person, characteristics or activities. Such a man cannot look except at the face of Allah, nor can he bow down before, hope for, or have fear of, anything other than Allah. He will not enjoy or be pleased with any other thing, nor will he rely on, or surrender to, anyone but Allah. In short, he will not desire or wish for anything except Allah - the Eternal One Who will remain when everything will perish; he will surely turn away from all the false-hood, that is, from everything other than Allah; he will not attach any importance to his own existence nor will he care for himself in face of the Absolute Truth, that is, the eternal existence of his Creator - Great is His Glory.

So there are many things that can help us to understand the emphasis on unity in Islamic thought. I will share only some of them very quickly, and then I will focus on some of them.

Islamic Philosophy

When it comes to Islamic philosophy, normally we have two major areas:

1)   Theosophy in its broadest sense *al-Ilāhīyāt bil-ma'na al-'āmm*. This is where we talk about the predicates or properties of being as being.

2)   Theosophy in its narrow sense *al-Ilāhīyāt bil-ma'na al-khāṣṣ*. This is where we talk about God.

The first area is about being as such, which applies to God and applies to contingent beings like us. So in philosophy we talk not about a specific being, but we talk about being as being.

Notion of existence in the Transcendent Philosophy

Muslim philosophers, especially Mullā Sadrā – who is the founder of Transcendent Philosophy (*al-ḥikmah al-muta'aliyah*) and has many books on philosophy, mysticism, and commentaries on the Quran and narration (*hadith*) very clearly established that everything in this world enjoys the same reality. Because there was and is a big question in philosophy: Where does multiplicity come from? We have human beings, animals, birds, nonliving beings, angels, so many things and we have God. How do you explain this multiplicity (*kathrah*) from a metaphysical point of view? For some people the idea was that they have different realities, but Mullā Sadrā in transcendent philosophy argued that we only have one reality, and that is existence. And the differences stem from a difference in the intensity of existence.

Thus a human being and an animal and a plant and a stone and angels, all have the same reality and that is existence. But we have different degrees of existence. Therefore, the result is that what makes us similar is what makes us different. It makes us similar because we have same reality and it makes us different because we have different degrees and intensity of that. For Mullā Sadrā, existence comes as, a ladder as a hierarchy. Each of us is a finite, limited being but we have different degrees. Then we have God, who is the absolute being. We are limited, but He is absolute.

So this perspective of the universe is a very important perspective because it puts you in a close and intimate relation with everything, and you do not differ in reality from each other; it is just a matter of degree. When it comes to human beings, their degree can vary depending on what they do or more precisely, what they are. Mullā Sadrā has the idea that human beings can actually be different in their species. All the horses are the same in degree and intensity of being even though they may look different. And all birds are the same, regardless of the type. But human beings can be totally different. This is a very important metaphysical approach to the issue of unity.

Notion of light in the Illuminationist Philosophy

The notion of light is one of those notions which are mentioned in the Quran and have inspired Muslim philosophers. For example, the notion of light has been used as the most fundamental notion in the Illuminationist Philosophy (*hikmah al-ishraq*) of Suhrawardi. He talks about different beings as different lights. I think what he says and what Mullā Sadrā says very much match each other. The Quran says: "*God is the Light of the heavens and the earth.*"[6] (The Qur'an, 24:35) Suhrewardī used this as the basis of his philosophy. The Quran also says that God created the skies and the earth and He also made light and darkness:

---

[6] The Arabic text is as follows:

اللَّهُ نُورُ السَّمَاوَاتِ وَ الأَرْضِ

23

All praise belongs to Allah who created the heavens and the earth and made the darknesses and the light.[7] (The Qur'an, 6:1)

Thus there are two ways of explaining creation. One is to say that we have the sky, earth, and different types of beings. Another way is to say that we have light and darkness. After careful reflection we realize that darkness is nothing except a lesser degree of light. So we only have light, but a lesser light, a less intense light compared to a higher light is darkness. So we do not have absolute darkness. Absolute darkness does not exist. Anything created by God has light, but we have different levels of light.

If you look at this you see there are lots of moral and even political ideas that can come out of this. If you believe the whole world is light but different levels of light, then the way you look at people will be different. This is because you can see the light of God in everything, but in certain things you can also see how they have turned away from God and created some darkness. So this is another concept.

---

[7] The Arabic text is as follows:

الحَمْدُ لِلَّهِ الَّذِى خَلَقَ السَّمَاوَاتِ وَ الأَرْضَ وَ جَعَلَ الظُّلُمَاتِ وَ النُّورَ

Everything is a sign of God

The other thing we find in Islamic thought is that everything is not only a creation of God but is also a sign of God. It might be possible to argue that nothing exists unless there is a sign for understanding it. We can even say that the reason God created us is in order to be known. There is a divine saying which says, "I was a hidden treasure and I wanted to be known, so I created people in order to be known."[8] To exist and to be known come together.

So everything is a sign of God. The Qur'an says that for you there are external signs – everything around us is a sign of God – and there are also internal signs:

> *Soon We shall show them Our signs in the horizons and in their own souls* (The Qur'an, 41:53)[9]

If we look at this – that everything is a creation of God and a sign of God – it means that everything is then somehow sacred. Sometimes I say that everything has a signature of

---

[8] *Biḥār al-Anwār,* vol. 84, p. 344. The original text is as follows:

كنت كنزا مخفيا فأحببت أن أعرف فخلقت الخلق لكى أعرف

[9] The Arabic text is as follows:

سَنُرِيهِمْ ءَايَاتِنَا فِى الآفَاقِ وَ فِى أَنفُسِهِم

25

God on it. If something has a signature of God on it, then can you disregard it? Can you destroy it? Some Muslim mystics are very hesitant to kill even mosquitoes or other insects. It has been said when the late Imam Khomeini was in Najaf, it was very hot and there were mosquitoes and flies but he never killed the mosquitoes. He used to use his cloak to send them outside his room.

There was a very pious scholar in Mashhad named Mīrzā Javād Aqā whose son said that once he was sitting in the courtyard of his house and wanted to go inside. When they saw him returning they asked him, What happened?" He said, "I saw some ants on my clothing and I'm going to the same place where I was sitting to leave them there so that they don't get displaced." For him, even an ant is significant.

If your father has many children, some of whom are top scholars or mystics and others who are normal people, all of them are important to you; you cannot say, "I love only that child of my father who is the best." We have to love everyone.

In Islamic spirituality we have to think that any creature of God might be better than me – even an insect can be better than me. There is a saying that God once asked Moses that the next time he has an appointment with God, to bring along someone who is worse than him. So Moses started looking around to find someone worse than him to take him with him. For a person like Moses who is spoken to by God, who is a prophet, it might be natural to think he is better than everyone so everyone is worse than him. But this was not his understanding. Whenever he looked at someone he thought "I cannot say they're worse than me. I cannot say I'm better than them." Then it is said that he found a very ill and very ugly dog, and he said I can't take any human being and say he's worse than me, maybe I can take this animal and say he's worse than me." But then he said "no, I cannot say I'm better than even this dog." Therefore he went to God and said "I couldn't find anyone worse than me." And God said "if you would have brought that animal, you would have lost your position." This approach gives you maximum respect to every sign of God. You would not be able except to wish them good, to respect them, and to love them.

One of the contemporary Muslim scholars who was a philosopher, mystic, and poet, who has also translated the Quran and is very famous, is the late Elāhī Qumsheī. It is said that he sometimes used to look at a flower and cry. For him a flower reminded him of God. Of course the beauty of a flower is not comparable to the beauty of God, but a flower can act as a window through which you can see God.

The face of God

Therefore we find here another very important concept, after the sign of God, the concept of the "face of God" or *wajhullah.* God does not have a body; He does not have hands or legs or a face. But the Qur'an – and also the Bible e.g. Psalms[10] – talks about the "face of God." What does this mean? For human beings, if I want to have maximum encounter with you, I should turn my face to your face. If I face this wall and you face that wall and we speak with each other, this is not maximum encounter. Or if I look at you and you turn your face away, this is not maximum encounter. For human beings, if they want to have maximum attention, they should turn their face towards what they want to attend to, and if they want to have an encounter it should be face-to-face. So face-to face is the best encounter.

Then the Qur'an says that if you want to have maximum encounter with God, there is no need to go around and find where God is facing so that you face His face. I do not need to go to the east or west to find where God is and find where He is looking at so that I go and try to face Him, and then have maximum encounter with Him. The Qur'an says:

> *Wherever you turn, the face of God is there.*[11] (The Qur'an, 2:115)

---

[10] For example, Psalm 105:4 reads as follows:

Seek the LORD and His strength; Seek His face continually.

[11] The Arabic text is as follows:

You have to sort out your own problem of not facing God. If you want to find God, you can find Him everywhere. But if you are not tuned towards God and if you are not turning your face towards Him, you cannot find Him anywhere. Therefore you can find God in holy sites – in the shrines, mosques, churches – you can find God even in markets, on the streets, everywhere, if you want to find God. Of course I am not saying these places are the same, but I am saying that it is possible to find God everywhere. But it is also possible to go to the holiest places and have no encounter with God. Not because God is not there, but because you are not turning towards God.

Thus we have this concept of turning your face towards God. And we also have the concept of seeking God's face: "Seeking the face of his Lord."[12]

Now, a question arises: who is a mystic? A mystic is not the one who just knows God. This is not the definition. Many people know God. A mystic is not the one who just knows God and loves God – no, it is more than this. A mystic is the one who is constantly able to see God. Nothing makes

---

فَأَيْنَمَا تُوَلُّواْ فَثَمَّ وَجْهُ اللهِ

12 The Qur'an, (92:20):

إِلَّا ابْتِغَاءَ وَجْهِ رَبِّهِ الْأَعْلَى

But only the desire to seek for the Countenance of their Lord Most High;

him forget God. All the time he finds God facing him. This is a mystic.

We have a saying from Imam Ali (a), our first Imam: "I have not seen anything without seeing God before it, after it, and with it."[13] If we have this approach, then in everything, every person, every moment, under any condition, we would be facing God. But this is not easy to achieve and not easy to maintain, because there are so many distractions, especially nowadays we live in the world of distractions, all kinds of distractions, including the internet, mobiles, SMS- all these things. How can a mystic achieve and maintain this condition of always turning towards God, nothing distracting him from God? For sure this is not something easy, but it is possible. The Qur'an says that there are people whom neither business nor merchandise makes them forget God.

> *by men whom neither trading nor bargaining distracts from the remembrance of God,*[14] (The Qur'an, 24:37)

---

[13] *Sharh 'Usūl Kāfī (Sadra),* vol. 3, p. 432. The original text is as follows:

ما رأيت شيئًا إلا وقد رأيت الله قبله وبعده ومعه

[14] The Arabic text is as follows:

رِجَالٌ لاتُلْهِيهِمْ تِجَارَةٌ وَ لاَبَيْعٌ عَن ذِكْرِ الله

In what follows, I will refer to what, in my thought, might be stages that we would go through in getting nearer to God or getting to the point that we would be able to remember Him constantly.

First, we start with believing in God and worshipping God. Many believers remain at this stage; they believe in God and they worship God, they go to the places of worship, they do certain acts of worship – they pray, fast, give alms, etc. But this is the minimum. The Qur'an says:

> I did not create the jinn[15] and the humans except
> that they may serve Me[16] (The Qur'an, 51:56)

Many people translate or interpret the verse as *"except that they may worship Me"* but I think this is not the best interpretation. Grammatically, the term *liya'budūn*[17] can mean "in order to worship Me," but it can also mean "in order to serve Me." Then this takes us to a new realm. We have the realm of the worshippers of God and we have the realm of the servants of God. There's a big difference between worshipper (*'ābid*) and servant (*'abd*). Of course not in the

---

[15] Jinns are a type of creature that has free will but is not as strong as human beings intellectually. This is different from human genes.

[16] The Arabic text is as follows:

وَ مَا خَلَقْتُ الجِنَّ وَ الانسَ إِلا لِيَعْبُدُون

[17] The original Arabic word in the verse.

modern sense of the term servant, but "servant" in the theological sense, someone who serves God. You can start worshipping God immediately after embracing faith, but to reach the point where you can be a servant of God, that is something that even after many years you may not achieve.

When it comes to our way of understanding, in every prayer we say, "I bear witness that Muhammad was a servant of God and a messenger of God."[18] He was a "servant of God" in the way that he believed, practiced, and lived; and he was a "messenger of God" in the way that God rewarded him. God made him a messenger because he was a servant. Therefore we do not say, "I bear witness that Muhammad was a worshipper (*'ābid*) of God." That's not a great achievement. We say, "I bear witness that Muhammad was a servant (*'abd*) of God." And we believe that this is the maximum a human being can achieve: to become a true servant of God. We cannot gain anything greater or higher than this.

We have a prayer from our first Imam which says:

> O my Lord, it is sufficient for me as a matter of honor and dignity to be Your servant, and it is sufficient for me as a

---

أشهد أن محمد عبده ورسوله

matter of pride that You are my Lord. I love you and I am very happy with You, so please make me in a way that You love.[19]

So this shift from being a worshipper to being a servant is a very big shift. You cannot become a servant if you have an ego because the Qur'an says that many people who have an ego are in reality serving their own ego instead of serving God: *"Have you seen him who has taken his desire to be his god?"* (The Qur'an, 25:43)[20]

There are two types of idol-worshippers. There are idol-worshippers who very explicitly go and worship a statue, and then there are many believers who are also idol-worshippers, but the idol is inside of them – they worship themselves.

A very clear example is Satan. Satan was a worshipper of God. He was very consistent; he worshipped God for 6,000 years, to the extent that some angels even envied him. It has been even said that when God was going to test the angels by asking them to prostrate before Adam, they knew that

---

[19] *Al-Khisāl,* vol. 2, p. 420. The original text is as follows:

إِلَهِى كَفَى بِى عِزّاً أَنْ أَكُونَ لَكَ عَبْداً وَ كَفَى بِى فَخْراً أَنْ تَكُونَ لِى رَبّاً

أَنْتَ كَمَا أُحِبُّ فَاجْعَلْنِى كَمَا تُحِبُّ

[20] The Arabic text is as follows:

أَرَأَيْتَ مَنِ اتخَذَ إِلَهَهُ هَوَاه

one person was going to fail. All the angels were worried, thinking, "Maybe I'm going to be the one who fails." So they would go to Satan and ask him to pray for them, and Satan would tell them, "Don't worry, I will pray for you!" And then he himself was the one who failed.

So worshipping God can become a habit, and after some time the difficulties go away because it is a habit. Then you start enjoying worship. You worship God because you enjoy it, not because you serve God. And when God asks you to do something else, you say, "No, I am enjoying my worship." There is a narration which says that when God told all the angels as well as Satan (he was with them at the time because of his worship) to prostrate before Adam, Satan said if You exempt me from this I will worship You in a way that no one has ever worshipped You, and God told him do you want to worship Me in the way that you choose, in the way that you like?[21]

Many of us gradually create a comfortable world for ourselves where we can keep our ego but pretend that we are servants of God. We are not servants of God. We are

---

21 *Qisas al-Anbiyā' li al-Rāwandī*, p. 43. The original text is as follows:

عَنِ الصَّادِقِ (ع) قَالَ: أُمِرَ إِبْلِيسُ بِالسُّجُودِ لآدَمَ فَقَالَ يَا رَبُّ وَ عِزَّتِكَ
إِنْ أَعْفَيْتَنِي مِنَ السُّجُودِ لآدَمَ ع لَأَعْبُدَكَ عِبَادَةً مَا عَبَدَكَ أَحَدٌ قَطُّ
مِثْلَهَا قَالَ اللَّهُ جَلَّ جَلالُهُ إِنِّى أُحِبُّ أَنْ أُطَاعَ مِنْ حَيْثُ أُرِيد

just worshipping God. This is the same mentality of those who do not believe in God. It is the same mentality, but some of us we think we are clever; we deceive God. We do our own selfish things but then we ask God to reward us: God, I am doing this for Your religion! I am doing this for You! But in reality, it is all the same business that even the people who do not believe in God were doing. Now we do it in the name of God, in the name of religion, in the name of scripture which might be very destructive.

What we need to do is to start with worshipping God and then try to do everything in order to please God. This is different from only worshipping God, because maybe pleasing God in a particular moment requires me not to go to the mosque and perform an act of worship and instead help someone on the street. Unfortunately, many times we deprive ourselves from great opportunities because we have focused and fixed our mind on something that we believe will take us to God, not knowing that great opportunities can come on the side. I thought about this often when I was in Qom. Let's say I am driving to go to the shrine to say a recommended prayer there and pay my visit, and I have a very limited time – I have to be quick. Sometimes I might see a mother with a child on the street waiting for someone to give them a lift, because in Iran it's very common. We use ride in other people's cars and we give lifts to each other. If I'm not a careful person, I would just ignore them. If I am a careful person, though, I would say I wish I could help them but God knows I am in a hurry, I have to go and pray. But if you are really alert, then you will say maybe now (maybe, I am not saying always) I have to give up my idea of going to the shrine and just help them, maybe this will be more pleasing to God.

Some people go to pilgrimage many times, even though going to Mecca just once is obligatory. It is good to go as often as you can but sometimes maybe in my family, among my friends, in my community there are people who do not have money. They are very poor. If I help them it would be more pleasing to God, but I still want to go to pilgrimage. We have to be very careful that in doing everything, we are seeking the pleasure of God, the face of God. So this is the second step. Then if we keep doing this, I think then we will reach a point where we would realize that I am a servant of God and my identity comes from God.

If you ask someone who thinks he has something to be proud of to explain his identity he will refer to that and will say: "I am a doctor, a professor, an engineer, or I come from this famous family." But if you ask a servant of the king, "Who are you?" if he is a true servant he will say, "I am a servant of the king." He will not say: "I am so-and-so," because for him so-and-so is not important. He will say, "I am a servant of the king." Similarly a servant of God always thinks that his identity comes from his belonging to God. The servant of God tells himself and others that I have a name, but that is not important. I have a job, I come from a certain family- those are not important. I am a servant of God.

If this comes to our mind that we belong to God, then I think it is a higher stage than trying to please God, because when you are trying to please God still you might have a kind of understanding of being independent of God. But on the other hand, you may try to please Him and then reach a point where you tend to forget yourself and just think that you belong to God; you become an agent of God.

If you are an agent of God and if you manage to get rid of your "self," which is like a shell, then it is easily possible to get united with others. As long as I am thinking of myself as a person, then I am different from you. But if I forget my personhood – if I forget my own independent identity – and try to get united in God and disappear in God, then there is no problem being united with you.

So a person who is selfless can easily get united with other selves. He has no problem. Maybe they have a problem because they still have a "self," like a shell. But this person has no problem because if we look at it from a philosophical perspective, each of us is like a container. A container does not have anything except that it comes from God. So if you have for example water in these containers, water comes from God. What comes from me is the shape and size which bring limitation. I do not have water of myself, I am just limiting. But I limited this size, you limited that size, I limited like a circle, you limited like a triangle – we are only limiting in ourselves the grace of God. But if we manage to get rid of our "self," then we will be connected to the ocean and we can easily get united with other people, if they want. You would have no problem. You can easily get united with them. You can understand them. Maybe they do not want to be with you, but that is not your problem. If a person really achieves this condition, then I think not only would he always be remembering God, he would also be able to remind people of God. Then this person becomes a godly person.

We have a narration (*hadith*) that Jesus' disciples asked him, "O Prophet of God, whom should we choose as our companions?" Jesus said:

> Those who remind you of God when you look at them, and they increase your knowledge when they speak, and when you look at their actions you become be more eager to work for your eternal journey."[22]

---

[22] *Al-Kāfī*, vol. 1, p. 39. The original text is as follows:

قَالَتِ الْحَوَارِيُّونَ لِعِيسَى يَا رُوحَ اللَّهِ مَنْ نُجَالِسُ قَالَ مَنْ يُذَكِّرُكُمُ اللَّهَ رُؤْيَتُهُ وَ يَزِيدُ فِى عِلْمِكُمْ مَنْطِقُهُ وَ يُرَغِّبُكُمْ فِى الآخِرَةِ عَمَلُهُ.

So a person is not only able to reach a point where he will never be distracted from God. Indeed, he can reach a point where he can help people get rid of distractions and be reminded of God. This is like a mirror that reflects the light of God.

I think the following analogy would help. Some people make us busy with themselves. For example, maybe you see good qualities in me and then you keep thinking about me and you keep praising me, and this can make you forget God. Some people say, "Please don't get stuck with me. God is over there." So they act as a sign. They say, "God is there." Other people are even more purified. When you look at them, you do not need to take direction from them to get directed to God; you look at them and in them you see God. So you are not stuck with them, but you meet them and you remember God. This is because they reflect very clearly the light of God. And this can reach a point where God makes them like a lantern. Every believer should be a mirror reflecting the light of God, but when it comes to for example, the prophets, they themselves are lanterns.[23]

---

[23] For example, the Qur'an says about Prophet Muhammad:

> O Prophet! Indeed We have sent you as a witness, as a bearer of good news and as a warner and as a summoner to God by His permission, and as a radiant lamp. (33:45 & 46)

If we at least reach this point and being at the stage of trying to please God everywhere and to seek the face of God everywhere, then I think we would be in a very good situation to unite with people. This is because the main obstacle for unity with people is the ego. That is, I think, the worst problem. And one of the worst types of ego may exist in religious people. For a person who does not believe in God or does not worship, his ego might come from his muscles – he might say, "I am very strong and you have to give me everything" – or his ego may come from his political party, or he may say, "I come from a royal family." But there is a limit to this. How much can you demand from people because of your muscles or because you belong to a party or because you come from a noble family? But for a person who has an ego and misuses God, there is no limit to what he can demand from people, because then he is saying that God is demanding this. He can even demand a person's life. He can say "It is God who demands this, not me. I can even take your life away from you. I can ask you to change your religion. I can ask anything of you, because it is not me but God."

So ego is the problem and the ego of religious people and religious leaders can be very dangerous because they are misusing the name of God. It is like a person who is very knowledgeable and does mischief compared to a person who is not knowledgeable. A knowledgeable mischief-maker can do more harm. Or for example, a person who has light in his hand and comes to rob your house compared to a person who comes in darkness and does not see anything. Even knowledge, even light, anything good- if it is misused, it can bring even more harm.

So we have to work on removing our ego from ourselves. We should not think that just because we are religious and worshipping God that we do not have an ego. There is a great chance that actually, in the same way that we are worshipping God we are growing our ego. Maybe the ego of an ayatollah or a bishop is much more than the ego of a first-year seminarian. You cannot say that because he is an ayatollah or a bishop he has no ego. It can grow.

So it is a constant struggle to make sure that we are not growing our ego through our faith and religiosity. Therefore I emphasize again on trying to always be thinking of the pleasure of God, not my own pleasure, and trying to find the face of God everywhere, not what I am used to. Maybe for me it is much easier to just meet my Muslim friends, my Shi'a friends. But is this what God would be happy with? That I only limit my contacts to my own people because it makes me more comfortable? Or maybe I never want to leave the seminary because I enjoy my studies. But is this what God wants from me? So we have to be very alert about this issue: whether we want to please ourselves or we want to please God.

Then there's a discussion, that maybe I will leave for tomorrow, about what in my understanding is the plan of God for guiding humanity. Why has God sent revelation and prophets? The way God wanted us to encounter revelation and the way we responded. I will leave it for tomorrow; God-willing we can discuss this tomorrow. Thank you very much.

God's Plan for Humanity in Creation: The One Human Family[1]

I am very grateful to God for giving us this opportunity of meeting again today and sharing our ideas about unity, its significance, and how to enhance it. Today, God willing, I will talk about the way I humbly understand the plan of God for humanity as portrayed in the Quran. I do not claim to have understood it completely or correctly, but it is after careful thinking and reflection over the years.

We can understand from the Quran that God's plan for humanity has been to unite around the truth – but voluntarily. He didn't want us to be forced to follow the truth and get united. He says, *"Had God willed, He would have He would have brought them together on guidance"* (The Qur'an, 6:35)[2] but He didn't want to force us. In Islamic theology, we

---

[1] This lecture was delivered on the 9th July 2016.

[2] The Arabic text is as follows:

وَ لَوْ شَاءَ اللَّهُ لَجَمَعَهُمْ عَلَى الْهُدى

distinguish between two types of will of God: "generative"[3] and "legislative."[4]

The generative will of God always materializes. Nothing happens in this world except by the will of God and through the will of God. Even for those who commit sins – those who disobey God – the generative will of God is there. Otherwise they are not able to do anything. They're not able to function. They're not able to exist. But this is the generative will of God.

We also have the legislative will of God, and that is those things that God asks us to do or not to do. He wants them to happen, but He doesn't force. Therefore, there are things that might happen against the legislative will of God, but not against the generative will of God.

God's legislative will is that humanity should be united around the truth. But God has offered this. He has invited us towards this. He has provided us with everything that we need for this – whether it be our moral conscience, our intellect, prophets, and revelation – everything that we need, God has given us. However, this is our test. This is something that we should do freely.

---

[3] *al-irādah al-takwīnīyah*

[4] *al-irādah al-tashrī'īyah*

Eventually, this is going to happen. Therefore there is no way for this world to end without that plan of God materializing. But God does not force His plan; He's patient. He leaves it to us to either make it happen or delay it. But eventually it is going to happen; it is just (a matter of) who is fortunate to be acting as agents for God and listening to the will of God and trying to implement the will of God. So, the ultimate end is that humanity will be united around the truth.

Unfortunately, we human beings have not responded positively to the invitation for unity. Even some of the things that God has given us in order to better relate to each other, we have used as a means for division. For example, in the Chapter 30 of the Quran mentioning some of His sign[5] God says:

> *And of His signs is that He created for you mates from your own selves that you may take comfort in them, and He ordained affection and mercy between you. There are indeed signs in that for a people who reflect.* (The Qur'an, 30:21)[6]

---

[5] It means something that you can reflect on and come to know God, one of the things that should lead you towards understanding God.

[6] The Arabic text is as follows:

وَ مِنْ ءَايَاتِهِ أَنْ خَلَقَ لَكُمْ مِّنْ أَنْفُسِكُمْ أَزْوَاجًا لِّتَسْكُنُوا إِلَيْهَا وَ جَعَلَ بَيْنَكُم مَّوَدَّةً وَ رَحْمَةً إِنَّ فِى ذَالِكَ لاَيَاتٍ لِّقَوْمٍ يَتَفَكَّرُون

God says that We have created you as male and female not to fight each other but to supplement each other. This is a wise plan of God that He has given us different genders to supplement each other. Then the next verse says that one of the signs of God also is the difference in your colours and languages:

Among His signs is the creation of the heavens and the earth, and the difference of your languages and colours. There are indeed signs in that for those who know. (The Qur'an, 30:22)[7]

This should take us towards God, not away from God through for example, fighting, declaring "we are better than you" or enslaving other ethnicities, and so on and so forth. No, the whole thing was to make this world more perfect, more beautiful, and easier to relate. In another verse God says:

O mankind! Indeed We created you from a male and a female, and made you nations and tribes that you may know each other. Indeed the noblest of you in the sight of God is the most pious among you.

---

[7] The Arabic text is as follows:

وَ مِنْ ءَايَاتِهِ خَلْقُ السَّمَاوَاتِ وَ الأَرْضِ وَ اخْتِلافُ ٱلْسِنَتِكُمْ وَ ٱلْوَانِكُمْ
إِنَّ فِى ذَالِكَ لَآيَاتٍ لِّلْعَالِمِين

Indeed God is all-knowing, all-aware. (The
Qur'an, 49:13)[8]

In the Qur'an sometimes God addresses the believers and
sometimes mankind. In this verse God is addresses mankind
and says that We have created you from a male and female
i.e. Adam and Eve, then We made you into different nations
and tribes. Why? So that you come to know each other. The
idea of creating us in different tribes and nations was to
come to mutual understanding and recognition, not to feel
that someone is superior to the other or that others are our
enemies. Then He says that the most honourable of you in
the sight of God are those who are more pious. Therefore,
language does not make you better. Colour, ethnicity,
gender- none of these make you better. It's only piety which
can make you better.

In the whole Quran there are only two things that I know of
which are mentioned as something that can raise someone's
position. One is piety and the second is knowledge. These
are very much connected. If you want to go higher, you have
to be more pious and you have to be more knowledgeable.
And both of them are in your hand. You can gain knowledge

---

[8] The Arabic text is as follows:

يَا أَيُّهَا النَّاسُ إِنَّا خَلَقْنَاكُم مِّن ذَكَرٍ وَ أُنثَى وَ جَعَلْنَاكُمْ شُعُوبًا وَ قَبَائِلَ

لِتَعَارَفُوا إِنَّ أَكْرَمَكُمْ عِندَ اللَّهِ أَتْقَاكُمْ إِنَّ اللَّهَ عَلِيمٌ خَبِيرٌ

47

– you can learn, you can seek knowledge, you can seek piety – but colour is not in your hand. Ethnicity is not in your hand. To which tribe you belong is not in your hand. So it's not fair or just to promote someone because of something that he has had no role, or to bring someone down because of something that he had no role.

Thus the plan of God was "to come to know one another." Imagine if in this room – although we are not that many – we all looked the same. How can we then recognize each other? And now if we have billions of human beings who were mass produced in the same shape, the same weight, the same colour, the same language – everything the same. We would not be able to know each other. We would not be able to identify each other. If, for example, all places in the world were the same, it would be boring. Therefore differences and diversity in creation is like different colours of a colourful mosaic, a colourful carpet, which makes it more beautiful. But unfortunately, we have seen in the history even some philosophers who have used differences in the human body to justify slavery. Even some Greek philosophers used to say that black people have a stronger body but white people have a stronger intellect, so it's natural for white people enslave black people. Even some religious people said slavery is fine. This is completely opposite to the plan of God.

Prophet Muhammad (s) said, "People are like the teeth of a comb."[9] You need different teeth, and maybe the size is different, but they supplement each other. In another hadith (narration) Prophet Muhammad (s) said:

> O people! Your Lord is one, your father is one. You all go back to Adam, and Adam was from soil. The most honourable of you are those who are the most pious and there is no privilege for Arabs over non-Arabs.[10]

God could have created us from different fathers and mothers, and still we should have been united because we have the same human nature and same creator. But God, to make us feel more united, created all of us from the same father and mother so that we feel we are members of the same family. This is an extra reason to feel united. So, your Lord is one, your father is one, Why do you feel you're superior to other people? There is no privilege for Arabs

---

[9] *Tuhaf al-'Uqūl*, p. 368. The original text is as follows:

النَّاسُ سَوَاءٌ كَأَسْنَانِ الْمُشْطِ

[10] *Tuhaf al-'Uqūl*, p. 34. The original text is as follows:

أَيُّهَا النَّاسُ إِنَّ رَبَّكُمْ وَاحِدٌ وَ إِنَّ أَبَاكُمْ وَاحِدٌ كُلُّكُمْ لآدَمَ وَ آدَمُ مِنْ
تُرَابٍ إِنَّ أَكْرَمَكُمْ عِنْدَ اللهِ أَتْقَاكُمْ وَ لَيْسَ لِعَرَبِيٍّ عَلَى عَجَمِيٍّ فَضْلٌ إلا
بِالتَّقْوَى

over non-Arabs, for red people over black people, the only privilege is God-fearing, piety.

Therefore the plan of God was to make human beings appreciate the commonalities that they have; the same humanity that we share, the same lord that we share, the same father and mother that they share. But unfortunately, people started to differ and fight. The Quran tells us that when people starting differing, God started sending the prophets with books:

> *God sent the prophets as bearers of good news and as warners, and He sent down with them the Book with the truth, that it may judge between the people concerning that about which they differed, and none differed in it except those who had been given it, after the manifest proofs had come to them, out of envy among themselves. Then Allah guided those who had faith to the truth of what they differed in, by His will, and Allah guides whomever He wishes to a straight path.* (The Qur'an, 2:213)[11]

---

[11] The Arabic text is as follows:

فَبَعَثَ اللّهُ النَّبِيِّينَ مُبَشِّرِينَ وَ مُنذِرِينَ وَ أَنزَلَ مَعَهُمُ الْكِتَابَ بِالْحَقِّ لِيَحْكُمَ بَيْنَ النَّاسِ فِيمَا اخْتَلَفُواْ فِيهِ وَ مَا اخْتَلَفَ فِيهِ إِلَّا الَّذِينَ أُوتُوهُ مِن بَعْدِ مَا

In brackets I want to mention something very important about the relation between religions and prophets. The Quran uses *"the Book"* (*al-kitāb*) in the singular form. It doesn't say "the books" (*al-kutub)*. It was natural to say "the prophets came with the books." But in many verses the Quran always says: "the prophets came with the Book" because there's one Book. According to the Quran, the books given to Abraham (puh), Moses (puh), Jesus (puh), Prophet Muhammad (puh) are not different books. Rather, these are different versions of the same Book; different editions and representations of the same Book. This is a very important concept for unity.

So God sent the prophets while they were giving the good news, the glad tidings and at the same time warning. If you do good, you'll be rewarded and if you do bad, you'll be held accountable. And God sent the Book with the prophets truthfully (*bilhaqq*). So that the Book would judge between people over what they disagreed. When the differences in opinions increased, there was a need for sending the Book. And the idea, the plan of God, was that this book should be followed and all the disagreements should finish. But what happened is now we have a second disagreement (*ikhtilāf*). People started disagreeing about the Book. *"none differed in it*

جَاءَتْهُمُ الْبَيِّنَاتُ بَغْيًا بَيْنَهُمْ فَهَدَى اللَّهُ الَّذِينَ ءَامَنُواْ لِمَا اخْتَلَفُواْ فِيهِ مِنَ الْحَقِّ بِإِذْنِهِ وَ اللَّهُ يَهْدِى مَن يَشَاءُ إِلَىٰ صِرَاطٍ مُّسْتَقِيم

except those who had been given it." God sent the Book to save them from some disagreement, but then the people said we understand the Book this way or that way. And most of the time, these were not genuine differences; they wanted to justify their own ways of thinking or ways of life. Therefore the Quran says that they did not disagree over the Book except after the Book was given to them and they had clear evidence, in order to treat each other with injustice. Then God guided those who had faith, who were real and true believers about the truth of which they differed. God guided the people who were true believers. And God guides those whom He wills to the Right Path."

We see how bad the response of humanity was. God saves them from one conflict and they start another conflict. They even start conflicting over what was supposed to give them unity! And the only way to be saved from this conflict is to be really, truly faithful; committed to the truth. This is very important for my discussion, this concept of truth. I'll come back to this.

When people differ over the Book, over revelation, over religion I think we can classify them into three groups.

I. Some people disagree and deny God and do not believe in religion and they show enmity to the believers. They fight against us. What should we do with enemies? The Quran says that you have to do a few things:

a. Without any exception, you must observe justice. You cannot be unjust, even to your enemies. So even if a person has killed my children, I cannot mistreat his children, or his family, or his people. The maximum is that the criminal should be brought to justice. But you cannot say "Because he has killed some of us, we do whatever we want with them because they are enemies; we burn them, destroy their town." No! Justice must be observed. The Qur'an says:

> *and let not the hatred of others to you make you swerve to wrong and depart from justice. Be just: that is next to piety: and fear God. For God is well-acquainted with all that ye do.* (The Qur'an, 5:8)[12]

Elsewhere in the Qur'an God says that do not let the hostility of the people of Mecca, the pagans who killed the Muslims, tortured them, confiscated their properties, and didn't let them go to the Ka'ba make you unjust.

> *and let not the hatred of some people in) once (shutting you out of the Sacred Mosque lead you to transgression) and hostility on your part.* (5:2)

---

[12] The Arabic text is as follows:

وَ لَايَجْرِمَنَّكُمْ شَنَانُ قَوْمٍ عَلىَ أَلا تَعْدِلُواْ اعْدِلُواْ هُوَ أَقْرَبُ لِلتَّقْوَى وَ
اتَّقُواْ اللَّهَ إِنَّ اللَّهَ خَبِيرُ بِمَا تَعْمَلُون

So the first principle with the enemies is justice. But the Quran says something more.

b. The Quran says that you should repel evil with not just something which is good, but something which is the best:

Repel evil with that which is best. (The Qur'an, 23:96)[13]

Therefore if I have an enemy who has done bad to me, the Quran prefers that we respond by doing what is the best. In another verse God expands on this and says that good and evil are not the same. If someone does bad to you, you should respond by doing the best. Thus the one with whom you have enmity becomes your close friend. Then the Quran says that no one is able to reach this point except those who have patience. It is not that everyone is able to respond to hostility with doing what is best.[14]

> *Good and evil] conduct [are not equal. Repel] evil [with what is best.] If you do so, [behold, he between whom and you was enmity, will be as*

---

[13] The Arabic text is as follows:

ادْفَعْ بِالَّتِى هِىَ أَحْسَنُ السَّيِّئَةَ

[14] The Qur'an, 41:34-35. The Arabic text is as follows:

وَ لَاتَسْتَوِى الْحُسَنَةُ وَ لَا السَّيِّئَةُ ادْفَعْ بِالَّتِى هِىَ أَحْسَنُ فَإِذَا الَّذِى بَيْنَكَ
وَ بَيْنَهُ عَدَاوَةٌ كَأَنَّهُ وَلِى حَمِيمٌ وَ مَا يُلَقَّهَا إِلا الَّذِينَ صَبَرُوا

54

though he were a sympathetic friend. But none is granted it except those who are patient, (The Qur'an, 41:34-35)

So there is no way to do injustice, and the preference is to do good in response to the bad. If this does not stop their enmity, you can defend yourself. But as much as possible, try to do good.

II. Some people disagree, they do not believe in religion, they do not believe in revelation but they are not enemies. We should not think that those who do not believe in religion are enemies of religious people. Some of them just do not believe. Because an enemy is the one who wants to harm you. A person who has made a mistake in his choice and does not believe in religion is not an enemy, as long as he does not want to harm you or destroy you.

So we have people who do not have faith but they are not enemies. What should be our response to them? The Quran says that with these people, you should have conversation without preconditioning:

Say: "Who gives you sustenance, from the heavens and the earth?" Say: "It is Allah. and certain it is that either we or you are on right guidance or in manifest error!" (The Qur'an, 34:24) [15]

God says to the Prophet (puh) that ask the people who deny God and do not believe in Him that who is giving you sustenance from the skies and the earth? And then tell them it's God who is giving you sustenance. But then God says that they may not accept this so tell them, "Either us or you are guided or misguided." This is very beautiful. It is God, and this is the Prophet, but God says "Tell them 'Either we or you are guided or misguided.'" This means that we don't presuppose that we are right and you are wrong. When it comes to God and the Prophet saying this, it leaves no chance for any believer to say "I am right and you are wrong." Even commentators of the Quran say that it would be enough to say "Either we or you are guided" or "Either we or you are misguided." But to add maximum flexibility God says "Either we or you are guided or misguided."

So you should be ready for conversation. And if it does not work, they do not listen, they insist- what should we do? Again here you should not fight them; tell them: *"To you be your Way, and to me mine."* (The Qur'an, 109:6) You follow your

---

[15] The Arabic text is as follows:

قُلْ مَن يَرْزُقُكُم مِّنَ السَّمَاوَاتِ وَ الأَرْضِ قُلِ اللَّهُ وَ إِنَّا أَوْ إِيَّاكُمْ لَعَلَى
هُدًى أَوْ فِي ضَلَالٍ مُّبِين

56

way of life and I follow my way of life. We do not fight them because they do not believe in religion or they do not believe in God.

IV. Then we come to the people who believe in God and revelation but they do not believe in the way that we do, they follow another religion, another tradition. When it comes to the people who do not believe in God at all, like pagans, we invite them for conversation. Therefore we can imagine that when it comes to for example Christians or Jews, it is not only "Let us have conversation without preconditioning." It is more:

> *Say, "O People of the Book! Come to a word common between us and you: that we will worship no one but God, and that we will not ascribe any partner to Him*, (The Qur'an, 3:64)[16]

The Qur'an says "Let's get together around the common word." You see that the language of the Quran changes.

---

[16] The Arabic text is as follows:

قُلْ يَأَهْلَ الْكِتَابِ تَعَالَوْاْ إِلَى كَلِمَةٍ سَوَاءٍ بَيْنَنَا وَ بَيْنَكُمُ أَلا نَعْبُدَ إِلا اللَّهَ
وَ لاَنُشْرِكَ بِهِ شَىْ

God's Plan for Humanity in Guidance: The Tradition of Abraham[1]

In this session what I want to share with you is some of my reflections on the verses of the Quran in which we see God's plan in guidance. In the previous session I talked mostly about creation and differences in the creation, but now I want to talk about religions and in particular about the Abrahamic tradition.

In the Quran, we find that Abraham has a very important position. To the extent that we can say Abraham is the founder of Islam. I had a series of 10 lectures in the shrine of the Lady Ma'sumah in Qom on this topic: "Abraham, the Founder of Islam." My understanding of the Quran – which I think is not very controversial but maybe people did not put it this way, but I think it is something that everyone would accept – is that God has not sent prophets with different religions. God sent prophets with the same book

---

[1] This lecture was delivered on the 9th July 2016.

and the same religion; it is people who historically gave different names to these religions.

There is only one religion. When the Quran says: "*Indeed, with God religion is Islam,*" (The Qur'an, 3:19)[2] this can be interpreted in two ways:

I. "Religion in the sight of God is only Islam" meaning there is no place for Christianity and no place for Judaism. There is only Islam which started 1,400 years ago. But I do not understand it this way. I understand it this (second) way.

II. There is only one religion, and that is submission to God. This is the religion of Abraham (puh), this is the religion of Jacob (puh), this is the religion of Moses (puh), Jesus (puh), and Prophet Muhammad (puh). This is the way I understand it, and in those lectures I have argued that our prophet did not bring a new religion so that we say "That's the only religion which is acceptable to God."

The Quran says that God tried and tested Abraham in different ways, and he was able to pass all of the tests: "*And when his Lord tested Abraham with certain words, and he fulfilled them,*" (The Qur'an, 2:124) And then God said, "*I make you the*

---

[2] Islam literally means submission and Muslim which is from the same root means submissive.

leader for mankind." (The Qur'an, 2:124)[3] By passing all these tests, Abraham reached pure unity of God. He's the champion of monotheism. And it is interesting that Abraham did not have a child for a long time and maybe had lost his hope – because when the angels gave the good news that he is going to have a child, he was surprised and his wife was surprised – but all the prophets actually come from Abraham. Abraham is someone who did not think that he would have even one child, yet all the prophets have come from him. We have Ishmael, and through Ishmael we have our Prophet (puh) and all our imams. And we have Isaac through whom we have Jacob and Joseph, and all the Israelites and Moses (puh) and Jesus (puh). They all go back to Abraham.

Therefore Abraham is not the only meeting point between Islam and Christianity; we share many prophets before. Abraham is our first meeting point. But also, Abraham is a champion of unity of God, and he articulated the unity of God in a very, very clear way.

---

[3] The Arabic text is as follows:

وَ إِذِ ابْتَلَى إِبْرَاهِيمَ رَبُّهُ بِكَلِماتٍ فَأَتَمَّهُنَّ قالَ إِنِّى جاعِلُكَ لِلنَّاسِ إِماماً
قالَ وَ مِنْ ذُرِّيَّتى قالَ لا يَنالُ عَهْدِى الظَّالِمينَ

God asked Abraham to restore the Ka'ba[4] in Mecca. Ka'ba was built before Abraham because the Quran says that it was the very first house built for humanity. *"Indeed the first house to be set up for mankind is the one at Bakkah,"* (The Qur'an, 3:96).[5] This is the House of God but also the house of humanity because anything which belongs to God belongs to humanity. It was destroyed and then Abraham restored it with Ishmael. And then God told Abraham, *"And proclaim the Pilgrimage among men"* (The Qur'an, 22:27)[6] to this place. When we go to pilgrimage, many of the things that we do are a restoration of what Abraham did. So in a sense God is asking us to remember what Abraham did. And not only Abraham- even some of the things that his wife did. For example, we go between the two hills of Safa and Marwa seven times. This is what the wife of Abraham, mother of Ishmael, was doing as she looked for water. So we even do what the wife of Abraham did exactly as she did it, because God wants us to remember Abraham as the champion of

---

[4] A cubic construction

[5] The Arabic text is as follows:

إنَّ أوَّلَ بَيْتٍ وُضِعَ لِلنَّاسِ لَلَّذى بِبَكَّةَ مُبَارَكا

[6] The Arabic text is as follows:

وَ أَذِّنْ فِى النَّاسِ بِالْحَجِّ

the unity of God. Out of His appreciation[7] for what Abraham did, and also to give us a lesson to follow, God says you go and put your step on the footsteps of Abraham.

What is the religion of Abraham? In some places the Quran says that the religion of Abraham is to submit your face to God. For example, the Quran says:

> *And who has a better religion than he who submits himself entirely to God? and he is the doer of good (to others) and follows the faith of Abraham,"*
> (The Qur'an, 4:125)[8]

So the religion of Abraham, which is also the religion of prophets before but Abraham very well established this, is to submit yourself to God and then on the ground, to do good things. I cannot say I have submitted myself to God and

---

[7] I would like to mention that God is very grateful. In the Quran we have this concept that might be new to you; once we had a discussion in Qom with American, Christian philosophers and I said that one of the titles of God is that He is grateful, and they said this is new. I don't know whether you have it or not. But God is grateful; it's impossible to do something purely and honestly and God would not thank you. Even the Quran says that God is very grateful; not only is He *shaakir*, or grateful, but He's *shakoor*, very grateful.

[8] The Arabic text is as follows:

وَ مَنْ أَحْسَنُ دِيناً مِمَّنْ أَسْلَمَ وَجْهَهُ لِلَّهِ وَ هُوَ مُحْسِنٌ وَ اتَّبَعَ مِلَّةَ إِبْرَاهِيمَ

حَنِيفا

then do bad things or do nothing. If you submit yourself to God, you have to do good things.

The whole concept of religion is this: submit yourself to God and do good things. This is the religion of Abraham, Moses, Jesus, Prophet Muhammad – all of them have the same religion. This is the core of faith. Even in some places the Quran says:

> *Surely those who believe, and those who are Jews, and the Christians, and the Sabians, whoever believes in God and the Last day and does good, they shall have their reward from their Lord,* (The Qur'an, 2:62)[9]

So you don't need to be a Muslim to go to heaven or to be a Jew to go to heaven or to be a Christian to go to heaven. If you are a believer in God and the hereafter, and you do good things, you can go to heaven. The main thing is, do you have submission to God or not? Maybe a Muslim doesn't have submission to God and he is claiming or pretending. Maybe a Christian has submission to God and out of his sincerity, this is what he thinks God asked him to do. The main thing is submission to God.

---

[9] The Arabic text is as follows:

إنَّ الَّذينَ آمَنُوا وَ الَّذينَ هادُوا وَ النَّصارى وَ الصَّابِئينَ مَنْ آمَنَ بِاللَّهِ وَ الْيَوْمِ الآخِرِ وَ عَمِلَ صالِحاً فَلَهُمْ أَجْرُهُمْ عِنْدَ رَبِّهِمْ

If this is the substance, the essence, the core of faith, then what would be the relation between a faithful Muslim and a faithful Christian? What's the relation between the two? In my understanding, they are not believers in two religions. They believe in the same religion; they are fellow religious people because religion is submission to God. A Muslim, a Christian, a Jew who is submissive to God – they don't follow different religions. Yes, maybe they follow different traditions, but it's the same religion!

We have some differences. But these differences, in my understanding, are mostly about how to submit yourself to God. For example, as a Muslim, I pray, I fast, I go to Mecca for pilgrimage, I give alms in the way that Islam tells me, I eat certain foods, I don't eat some foods, all as a matter of submission to God. Therefore these are the ways I submit myself to God. But what about a person who does all these things while his heart is not submissive to God? It's very possible. Actually, most religious people – no matter which religion they adhere to – are very good at doing rituals and sacraments, but their heart is not necessarily submissive to God.

Thus if someone has submission to God but the way he submits himself to God is different from the way I submit myself to God – meaning his code of law and my code of law are different – in my understanding, this is a secondary issue. The main thing is: let's submit ourselves to God, and then to the best of our understanding try to understand the best way to submit to God. But what is the point of fighting over how to submit to God and then having no submission?!

Now, how do you evaluate and weigh these two: submission to God and how to submit? For some people, how to submit is 99% of the religion, if not 100%. So as soon as they see that there are people who do different things, they say, "No, they're different from us," as if they don't have anything in common. Sometimes even people who follow the same religion but different denominations, think that they are totally different. But I think the whole idea of faith is submission to God. If someone has submission to God, then how to submit is secondary. Of course this is not something that you can give figures, but I can say that submission constitutes at least 90% (of religion). If you're submissive to God, it's 90%. How to submit is 10%. That 10% is very important. Even 1% is very important because you want the purest way of submission to God. But don't forget submission itself!

For example, if a person is truthful and he struggles to find out the truth about certain issue but mistakenly believes in something, morally he has no problem because he's truthful. But if someone is not truthful, even if he says the truth, this is not morally good. The Quran says something very beautiful about hypocrites. The Quran says:

When the hypocrites come to you they say, "We bear witness that you are indeed the Messenger of God." God knows that you are indeed His Messenger, and God bears witness that the hypocrites are indeed liars.[10] (The Qur'an, 63:1)

The hypocrites say *"you are the Messenger of God."* They don't say something wrong. They say the truth, but God says that they are liars. So truthfulness is not something that can be judged by what people say. Truthfulness is something that can be judged by looking at the heart of people. A person might be truthful but he doesn't know what to say, or maybe he says something mistakenly. For example, a truthful person may think that today [Saturday] is Monday and he says, "Today is Monday." We don't say (to him), "Because you said today is Monday you are a liar." No, he's a truthful person who made a mistake. But a dishonest person, even if he says the truth, is dishonest. He cannot hide behind the truth.

Therefore the main thing is submission to God, and this is only possible when it's in one's heart — not by what some people physically do or something they say. If there is a

---

[10] The Arabic text is as follows:

إِذَا جَاءَكَ الْمُنَافِقُونَ قَالُوا نَشْهَدُ إِنَّكَ لَرَسُولُ اللَّهِ وَ اللَّهُ يَعْلَمُ إِنَّكَ لَرَسُولُهُ وَ اللَّهُ يَشْهَدُ إِنَّ الْمُنَافِقِينَ لَكَاذِبُون

Muslim who is submissive to God or a Christian who is submissive to God, they are closer to each other than two Muslims, one of whom is submissive and the other is not; or two Christians, one of whom is submissive and the other is not.

We do not need to forget our differences. We do not want to compromise on those differences. Of course we can always discuss how to come to a better agreement, but even if you have all the differences, they are more about how to submit. Otherwise we don't have any doubt that we should submit ourselves to God. And all of us always try to find what God wants from us and try to submit ourselves to God. We would not rest until we make sure that we have submitted ourselves to God. So we don't have different religions; we have the same religion but just different ways of showing our practices and our way of submission.

The elements which help to unite religions

I. Spirituality

How can we get closer to this point? One requirement is spirituality. Unfortunately, some people take religion more as a matter of rituals, as a matter of law. These are certainly important aspects of religion and I do not want to underestimate them, but these are not the core of religion. And if you focus on these things then you have more differences. But if you go to the spirit of religion and try to empty yourself of your ego, and try to submit yourself to God, and have purity of heart, and purity of intention then you'll see that you will be able to better see the good things that other people have.

This is something that is very logical and as a matter of fact, you can see that mystics and spiritual people always show better relations with people of other faiths. It is very difficult to find a great mystic who is close-minded. Normally, spiritual people are more open, not because they are less pious; no, they may be more pious. But for them piety is not defined by performing some actions. If for you piety is performing some actions then you find you don't have anything in common because I pray one way and you pray another way. These do not define piety.

So the more spiritual we are, the more humble we are and the greater the chances that we will appreciate unity. And if you really love God, you would be more than happy to see other people sharing the same God with you. Some people feel worried if you say, "These people also worship the same God. These people also submit themselves to the same God." They say, "No! This is my God, not your God." But the people who are spiritual are the opposite; not only do they acknowledge the worship and praise of other believers, they even say, "Idol-worshippers praise my God, although they don't know it."

If you go for example to a Muslim mystic like Ibn Arabi, he says that no one other than God has ever been worshipped. Even idol-worshippers worship God but they don't know it. And he says that no one other than God has ever been loved. He says that if people love Zeinab and Su`aad (these are two Arabic names of women) if they love a woman, they really love God, but in that woman they see the beauty of God but they themselves do not understand. In reality every human being is searching for absolute beauty, and some people are pleased with mere finite beauty in a woman or another worldly matter. They forget God, but he says that they all unconsciously love God. You see the approach? This person is trying to say, "Everyone is with God" and in this way he wants to bring them closer to God, yet there are others who push people away from God, like for example what we have today in the Muslim world unfortunately – and the same in Christianity and Judaism – there are some Muslims (*takfiri*) who say even to Muslims, "You are infidels." They say that the Shi'a are kafir, and not only the Shi'a but many Sunnis are kafir! And they say: "these Shi'a and Sunnis should be killed and destroyed." They're ready to commit suicide and kill themselves so that they can kill one Shi'a and by killing one Shi'a they say you can go to heaven.

This comes from a lack of spirituality because if you really love God, you should say that these Shia are confused and misguided (according to them) – not more than that. Why push them away? 150 million Muslims in the world worship

God, pray, go to hajj, etc., why do you want to call them infidels? This comes from a lack of understanding and I think also a lack of humbleness and spirituality.

When you work for a corporation or organization, what do you hope to do? You try to bring everyone to your camp. You want to be active in marketing and bring people towards you. What type of people are these takfiris? They want to send all people away! They even caused an explosion in Medina! Can anyone understand how a Muslim explodes a bomb in Medina? Why does this happen? Because there is no spirituality, there is no humbleness. So spirituality, and especially the humbleness that spirituality brings, paves the way for understanding that unity between religions that we discussed earlier.

II. Knowledge

The second thing is knowledge. Those who have a comprehensive understanding of religion can better give everything its due weight and significance. It is impossible to know the different aspects of Islam, the different aspects of the Qur'an, and then just think that religion is equal to a few rituals. We see that for some people who are not very educated, something which is secondary, is considered a priority for them. There is a funny example. There was a time when the tomato was very new in Iran. Even today we call the tomato gojeh farangi, which means "a western plum." Some people took this as a kind of foreign invasion of culture. So one day a father saw that his young son came home and secretly brought something home with him. He was hiding it. The father checked and realized that his son brought some tomatoes with him. He was very angry. He said, "You didn't say your prayer and I kept silent, you didn't fast and I kept silent, but today I cannot keep silent! You brought tomatoes!" You see, eating tomato is more important for him than not saying prayers and not fasting – which are pillars. So those who don't have knowledge can take something which is important but a small part of religion, as their main principle.

We Muslims, Sunni and Shi'a, share the same God, the same Qur'an, we say prayer five times a day in the same direction, we fast, so many things! Yes, we have differences too, but why have those differences become more important than these commonalities? In the same way, we Muslims and Christians share the same God and we try to submit ourselves to the same God – the God of Abraham – why do we place so much emphasis on our differences that it overshadows our submission to the same God, which I think is the core of religion? I do not want to say that we should forget our differences, but I am saying we should not put too much emphasis on what divides us.

If you look for example at the history of the church in Europe, there was a time when Protestants and Catholics used to fight each other. And they were not saying, "We are different Christians who differ." They were saying, "We are the only Christians and you are not Christians." The same problem we have today with these ISIS people who say, "We are the only Muslims and you are not Muslim." So there was a time when Catholics and Protestants used to think, "We are the only Christians and others are not Christians. They're heretics."

Today I don't think you've managed to solve all of your disagreements, but your understanding of the greatness of Jesus and the Bible has convinced you that we can be celebrating our common Christianity and still be accepting my Catholic tradition or you accept your Protestant tradition "I don't want to become Protestant and you don't want to become Catholic, no problem." But, "I recognize you as Christian and you recognize me as Christian." So what has changed? Differences have not been solved and did not disappear. The only change is a change in the way you measure differences. If you focus on the areas in which you differ, then you'll find that you have nothing in common. But if you have a broader perspective, then you'll see that you have differences but you also have lots of things in common.

Now if we Muslims and Christians broaden our vision and try to submit ourselves to God, we will realize that those differences are not as big as we think today. We are following the same tradition of Abraham and that is submission to God.

III. Emotional growth

So, spiritual growth helps. Growth in knowledge and understanding helps. Emotional growth also helps. If you are a loving character, if you are a passionate character, even this shows itself in your theology. And if you are a person who in his personal life is not a loving character, this also reflects in your theology. For people with big hearts who love more, when it comes to interreligious relation, dialogue, and theology, they can better open their hearts to accommodate others.

If you have been brought up in a loving family, environment and when you were growing, your parents and your environment have given you lots of love, then when you become a theologian or religious leader, you may reflect this love on other people. If you have been connected to God and receive love from God, you reflect this on people. God says to Prophet Muhammad (s) that because you have received mercy from God, you have become a soft person:

It is by God's mercy that you became softened to them.[11] (The Qur'an, 3:159)

It is impossible for someone to get closer to God and becomes arrogant, becomes harsh, becomes aggressive. Unfortunately, some people mistakenly think that if they are more spiritual, they should not smile or meet people. No, the Prophet was the closest person to God and he was a very easy-going person. Even the hadith says that many old women used to stop the Prophet in Medina to tell him things – some people who become old like to talk more – and the Prophet never told them, "Hurry! I have to go."[12]

Children would also go to the Prophet. We have an incident where some children in Medina asked the Prophet to play with them. The children told the Prophet – who was with some of his companions – "You should play with us; if you play with your grandchildren you should also play with us." The Prophet didn't say, "I am a prophet, I don't play with children." Or he didn't say, "I'm in a hurry, people are waiting for me in the mosque." No, he started playing with them and sent (his companion) Bilal to bring something

---

[11] The Arabic text is as follows:

فَبِما رَحْمَةٍ مِنَ اللَّهِ لِنْتَ لَهُمْ

[12] Makarim al-Akhlaq, p. 15. The original text is as follows:

مَنْ تَكَلَّمَ أَنْصَتُوا لَهُ حَتَّى يَفْرُغَ حَدِيثُهُمْ عِنْدَه

from home. After Bilal brought some walnuts, the Prophet asked the children, "Are you happy to take these walnuts and release me?" They said, "Yes." Then the Prophet said, "I was sold cheaper than Joseph."[13]

This is a man of God that people can meet and talk to him without worry. It reached the point where some people began to criticize the Prophet. In chapter 9, the Quran says: *"Among them are those who torment the Prophet, and say," He is an ear."*[14] (The Qur'an, 9:61) They would say that he is just an ear! This man just listens to us! It's very difficult to receive revelation and still let people talk to you, without rushing them and without asking them to stop.

If you have a loving character, this paves the way for you in interreligious relations; you can be a better ambassador for unity because we're human beings, we're not robots. What is in our heart affects what comes into our mind or onto our tongue. The Quran says, *"Everyone acts according to his character."*[15] (The Qur'an, 17:84)

---

[13] http://www.islamquest.net/fa/archive/question/fa22844

[14] The Arabic text is as follows:

وَ مِنْهُمُ الَّذِينَ يُؤْذُونَ النَّبِيَّ وَ يَقُولُونَ هُوَ أُذُنٌ

[15] The Arabic text is as follows:

كُلٌّ يَعْمَلُ عَلَى شَاكِلَتِهِ

IV. Attacks against religion

The fourth element which helps unite religions is attacks against religions. I think today we have lots of attacks against all religions. Sometimes attacks are directed at one aspect of a particular religion. For example, some people might criticize hijab (i.e. head-covering) in Islam. Some people might criticize the requirement of celibacy among Catholic priests. These are attacks on particular issues in different religions. But sometimes the attack is not directed at hijab or celibacy or something else; rather, the attack is on the whole idea of why we should submit ourselves to God. Today the culture of liberalism and secularism suggests to people that you don't need to please God, just please yourself, just enjoy yourself. Do what you like and just be careful not to get yourself into trouble. Is this a problem only for Muslims? Is it a problem only for Christians? Or is it a problem for everyone who believes in God and tries to submit himself to God?

There are forces working very hard against any concept of holiness and sacredness, and they want to de-sanctify everything. So the attacks have started at the surface – from the shell and the peal – and have reached the core of faith. Today the whole idea of faith and submission to God is under attack. I always say to my Muslim brothers and Christian brothers that my problem today in London for example, is not that Muslims become Christians or Shi'a become Sunni. No, I do not have such problems and worries. My problem is people leaving aside the whole idea of faith! The problem of destruction of families, the problem of people leaving their wife and children without feeling a sense of responsibility, people getting addicted, for example. Of course, in my community thank God these problems are less but they still worry us. I am always worried to hear news about divorce or separation.

These are our problems. You feel the problem is not Muslim becoming Christian. The problem is people forgetting God. So now that there is such an attack against us, in a sense this can be an opportunity to realize, to wake up – to realize that we have to work together, because this is the whole idea of faith.

Unfortunately, sometimes people generalize the problems that exist in some locality. For example, maybe in some places like Indonesia, Malaysia, or some places in Africa, there is rivalry between Muslims and Christians. But this should not make Muslim and Christian leaders and thinkers think that the problem in the world is between Islam and Christianity. If you look at the world at large, I see we do not have problem between Islam and Christianity; Islam and Christianity are working together. We are brothers and sisters and we are under the same attack. But this needs someone to have a global vision. Otherwise if I have a problem with my Christian neighbour, then I will think that in the whole world problem is between Muslims and Christians.

In the past Islam and Christianity have sometimes cooperated, especially in scientific, scholarly issues. For example, in the medieval ages there was a lot of collaboration and exchange. But I think in religious activities, in calling people towards God there has not been much collaboration in our history. Generally speaking, Christians did whatever they did on their own and Muslims on their own. Christians managed to spread Christianity and Muslims managed to spread Islam, but I think it is wrong to think that this can continue in the future. The pressures against religion, the pressures against submission to God, are so high that there is no way for us to continue without working together. We should not get stuck in history. The only way forward for us is to invite people to the beauty of faith together, in a united way. Then there is a chance that we may be able to overcome the spread of atheism, liberalism, and secularism.

If we do not work together, the pressures are so high that each of us will be victims separately. For example, when wolves attack while the cattle are scattered, they become easy targets. I am very sad to see that still today in the world, there are Christians who spend their time and energy criticizing Islam and there are Muslims who do the same to criticize Christianity. Does God really want me to spend my time finding a mistake in the Bible? Does He want Christians to spend time finding a mistake in the Quran? Is this what God wants from me today? While there are people who don't believe in God at all! And they are growing and spreading.

Our families are breaking down, some of our children are either turning to extremism or prison or not going to the church or Mosque. We are forgetting all of that and we keep the historical business of attacking each other. This is wrong. I think now these pressures are enough to awaken every person and make us motivated to join our efforts, to join our resources, to collaborate – and in this way get closer to God, closer to the core of faith, and also to serve humanity.

Humanity is very much in need of seeing our unity. There are many people who love to see us fight each other because then they can say, "Look at these faithful people, they're trouble makers! Wherever there are religious people, they bring tension and problems. We shouldn't have Muslims in this country because then we'll have Muslims and Christians fighting," or "We shouldn't have Christians in this country because then we'll have Christians and Muslims fighting." Unfortunately, this is the idea that you get from many media outlets.

And some people say, "Let's get rid of all religious people" or "Let them confine religion only to private sphere; if you want to have peace, if you want to progress, we should have no presence of faith in the public sphere." So what should we do? Should we give them excuses? Should we fight each other? Boycott each other? No, we should show them how our faith has united us, how our commitment to God has made us brothers and sisters. And then they will be encouraged to try faith in God.

But this also needs something very important: to realize what is the core of faith. I think many people have this problem. I say it very boldly, for many people it's not very important whether people are submissive to God or not; it's important whether they are Muslims or not, whether they are Christians or not. But I think this is wrong. If people who have no faith become Christians, I become very happy and I should do everything possible to help them come to faith in God. In what form is a secondary issue. But if we are attached to our faith in a way that we make it more important than God, then that's dangerous.

Sometimes I think when we want to "get to the gold" – as Piero was saying, or as we say in Islamic mysticism that when we want to reach the reality, the truth, which is the *lubb*, like the pearl that has a shell around it and you have to peal it to reach the core – there are many things that you have to leave aside. I have to leave aside my nationality, not in the sense that I quit my nationality, but in the sense that I don't worship my nationality. (I have to leave aside) my gender, my language, my colour, my tribe, my city. Anything that can be an issue that makes you forget God should be left aside, because then these become idols – my fame, my job, my position.

And I think one of the very last things that can be a veil or barrier between us and God is religion. But please don't get me wrong. This has the potential of being very much misunderstood. Religion is to bring us to God, not to become God. Religion is to serve us to reach the truth. If for me, my attachment to religion is more important than God or the truth, then that's the problem! This is not pure monotheism (*tawhid*). We should be able to penetrate through all the veils (*hijab*). Sometimes my knowledge can be my veil. Sometimes my cleric position can be my veil. Sometimes being a Shi'a or Sunni or Catholic can become a veil. But a person who is submissive to God, the absolute truth, and nothing other than reaching God satisfies and pleases him, whenever he has to choose between God and anything else, he chooses God, even if that thing is religion.

Again I say that this can be misunderstood. If it's not clear what I mean please ask me, because there's a great chance of being misunderstood. I am not against religion. I am a religious person and I am ready to die for my religion. But I am saying that I would never sacrifice God for the sake of my religion. If my religion is a good religion, it should help me serve God – not that I serve my religion. I serve only God.

So what is important is to move to the end of the plan of God for religion and guidance, and then tomorrow I'll talk about the way we can work for that. [...] Thank you very much.

God's Plan for End of the Time[1]

First, I thank God the Almighty for the beautiful time that we have had together and ask Him to remove any obstacle in our way towards unity, whether it be an obstacle inside us or outside of us.

It is difficult for me to decide what to talk about. There is a remaining part of my talk yesterday about the plan of God for guidance and what humanity should achieve voluntarily – although it is voluntarily, it will eventually happen – and about some suggestions for enhancing Muslim-Christian relations, and also about how there should be unity and mutual love between believers. So there are three areas and it's difficult for me to choose which one to give preference to.

I start with a brief discussion about the plan of God for the End of Times. I start with a reflection that came to mind in Loppiano when Mahnaz and Israa and other women came

---

[1] This lecture was delivered on the 10th July 2016.

here in February-March of 2015. We visited some priests of the movement in the church. We were originally going for a short visit and then one of the older priests asked us to drink something. We said, "Yes." But that was not the first choice if it was a personal choice, because the first choice was to go (since we had to leave), but we said that we should say yes to this invitation. Thanks to God, we sat around the table and some of the most beautiful reflections I had in the recent years came there. Then Paul (Lemarie) who was there said, "Do you allow me to record?" so he started recording. Then after that, for the rest of the time we were here (in Loppiano) he was recording, but it started over there. I say this not in order to say that I am special, but just to say that I am not special. It is a gift of God that can come and you do not own it. It just comes. It is not mine. I owe it to that moment.

So I said in that meeting with the priests of the movement that to me, it seems very clear and very much in line with Islamic theology, that God sent different prophets and these prophets spoke to human beings who were the same in nature but belonged to different cultures. They spoke different languages, they had difficult situations, and they had to address these difficulties. Although the message was the same, it took the shape and form of each community that the prophets addressed. Like water, for example, that comes from the same source but then goes to different lakes or even containers. It can take different shapes and forms, but we should not forget that it is the same water.

So now what we have is that some people have taken those shapes and forms as more important than the water. We say, "We are Muslim" "We are Christian" "We are Jewish" or "We are Sunni, Shi'a, Catholic"- all these are shapes and forms, which are very important, but this is not the most important thing.

Imam Mahdi and Jesus come together

We believe that in the End of the Time our 12th Imam, Imam Mahdi, will come and he will be accompanied by Jesus. They have a universal mission which is to establish justice and equity on the Earth. And I think at that time it will not be that our 12th Imam has a mosque in which he addresses people and Jesus has a church to address people, or that our Imam has a school where he teaches Islam and Jesus has another school where he teaches Christianity. I think in the End of Times there will be one school, and that is the School of God in which Jesus and our Imam teach, representatives of different divine traditions can teach – but it is all dedicated to God the One, who is the God of everyone. Shapes and forms will no longer divide us. They would simply help us to better recognize each other, like different colours of humanity, different races.

And then I said that when I reflect on Islamic sources about the people who will be qualified to be agents of God to implement that plan, I can see that those qualities exist – to some extent – in my Focolare friends. I do not feel bad to say that I can see the qualities that must exist in the helpers of the 12th Imam in my Focolare friends more than I can see them in myself or in some of my people.

Some qualities of the companions of Imam Mahdi

We find that in a hadith from Imam Ali (a) in which he mentions a few qualities about the people of the End of Times who will help the 12th Imam in his universal mission. One is that they are very determined: "If they decide to move mountains, they will do it."[2] And then he says that although they come from different parts of the world, when you look at them you think that they're "brought up by the same father and the same mother."[3] In addition, "Their hearts are united with love and wishing good for each other."[4]

---

[2] *Ilzām al-Nāsib*, vol.2, p. 165. The original text is as follows:

لو أنّهم همّوا بإزالة الجبال الرواسى لأزالوها عن مواضعها

[3] Ibid. The original text is as follows:

كأنّما ربّاهم أب واحد و أمّ واحدة

[4] Ibid. The original text is as follows:

I said that I can see in the Focolare friends that they have this quality, that when you look at them you think that they are brought up by the same father and mother. This is something that I have observed carefully over the years. It is now maybe 19 years – and at that time maybe 17 years – that I have known the Focolare, in different places like in the UK, the US, Canada, Lebanon, Italy, Poland, Philippines. I have met the Focolare in many places and I can feel that it is as if they're brought up by the same father and mother and their hearts are united with love.

So that plan of God which is to have unity around the truth, to reach the point where people will go to the School of God with one syllabus, one education system, needs such people, people who have been united among themselves and they can also offer this unity to other people.

Lake and ocean of united drops

In Mariapolis last year in the UK, I said that human beings are like drops of water; each human being is a drop of water. And in Christianity it is said that every human is created in the image of God. So in this drop of water which is very little, you can still have a reflection of God. Like for example, if you have a drop of water and the sun is shining, the light can be reflected. That is little compared to the

قلوبهم مجتمعة بالمحبّة و النصيحة

greatness of God. But if these drops of water unite, you will have a lake. The way this lake acts as an image of God is very much different from individual drops of water; the way in which a united humanity can act as an image of God is much more than individuals. And to me, the Focolare is a beautiful lake of united drops. But we should reach the point where we have united all of humanity.

The example of the Focolare shows that it is possible to have this unity, people coming from different parts of the world, speaking different languages, having different customs, having different lifestyles. Everyone has a different baggage with himself, but they are able to unite. This is possible but it has to be offered to humanity. So we have a lake but we need an ocean of unity. I do not know whether this lake will grow and become an ocean, or whether other lakes will take form and then merge to become an ocean. We do not know, but we have to reach that ocean. And we need to appreciate this lake because at the moment this is an example, and people need to see an example. If you give hundreds of hours of talks but you are not able to show a sample, people will think that this is not possible. But this example shows that it is possible.

Human beings are like one body

Then I said to the priest that another thing we find in Islam is that the believers should be like one body. There is a famous saying of our Prophet (s) that the Iranian poet Sa'dī made into a poem and this poem is also displayed on the wall of the United Nations headquarters in New York. The Prophet (s) said that the example of the believers in their mutual love, mutual affection, and sympathy, is like one body. If one part of the body has a problem, the rest of the body will show sympathy by having a fever or not being able to sleep.[5] If you have pain for example, in your head or ear, it is not that the rest of the body says, "We'll go to sleep and you keep awake." Instead, the whole body aches with fever and sleeplessness.

Circulation of blood in the body

I was reflecting on this in a meeting that we had with some of our graduates of the Jāmiat al-Zahrā, an Islamic seminary for women. Some years back, we had a meeting for our alumni from different countries and I was sitting and we had a guest who was speaking. I was listening to him but I was also thinking about the significance of such a meeting where we have women from tens of countries who have left their homes and families to come to Qom to study. They stayed for a few years in Qom and then they went back home, and now again they have come back here for a meeting of

---

[5] *Nahj al-Fasāhah*, p. 382. The original text is as follows:

تری المؤمنین فی تراحمهم و توادّهم و تعاطفهم کمثل الجسد اذا اشتکی

عضوا تداعی له سایر جسده بالسّهر و الحمّی

91

alumni. So I was thinking about the significance of this meeting while remembering the *hadith* of the Prophet (s) that the believers are like one body. Then it came to my mind that if we are part of the same body, a body has this quality that you have a circulation of all the goods; the heart pumps blood to all cells of the body. Each cell takes what it needs and puts in what it can share. So if there is something good produced by one organ of body, they put it in the blood and it reaches all the cells. And if they need, they take. If we are ill, maybe one part takes more and then it becomes ill. But if we are healthy, every part takes the oxygen and food that it needs, and leaves the rest.

This circulation is so nice that even the cell that is farthest from the heart will receive it; it is not that it will be forgotten. It is also not one-way that the centre sends without receiving feedback, without receiving ideas. That reflection led to a very important discussion for me about the collective nature of *wilayah*. So the next day I travelled to Tanzania and I met Shia preachers in East Africa, and for first the time I gave a lecture about the collective nature of *wilayah*, which I think is very important for understanding the unity of humanity. I really did not know whether they would appreciate my talk or if they would totally disagree, but I gave them the talk and everyone welcomed it. At night, one of the Shi'a in Dar es Salam (Tanzania) told me that you will see the result of this talk in ten years.

Anyway, that's one line of thinking and I have given lots of lectures about that collective nature of *wilayah* which I think is a missing part of our faith, because unlike what Islam teaches us and what our Shi'a Imams teach us, we normally have taken *wilayah* as a personal relation with God and the Imam, while everything suggests that *wilayah* is our relation with each other and God and the Imam. So we don't have parallel relations; we have one relation. This is a very important change in our mindset. Anyway, I'll leave that aside.

Going back to the discussion with the priest, that reflection about the human body and circulation- I said to the priest that I think in my observation of the Focolare Movement, there is such a circulation. Over the years I have been observing these things. Many movements and organizations are normally one way. For example, the leadership says something and everyone is going to do it; there is no mutual communication. But among the Focolare what I noticed was that things always go and come. It was for example, very interesting for me to know that the leader, for example Chiara, every month held a telecommunication with people of the movement all over the world and they discussed everything together. Every year responsibles of the movement come for three weeks to Rome. They do some prayer and contemplation, and then they start discussing everything together. And this goes for all levels; when Word of Life is sent, every community sits together and discusses, and this goes back and forth.

This is the same thing our Prophet (s) is saying, that the believers should be like one body. I think this type of model of unity will have a great role to play in the End of Times.

Why does Imam Mahdi (a) come with Jesus (a)? As a Shia I have to find an answer to this question. Of course, this is an Islamic idea, not only a Shi'a one, but for the Shi'a it's very important because we are very much attached to Imam Mahdi (a), although Sunnis also have the doctrine of Mahdi. For you as Christians it is very natural that Jesus (a) should come, but for me as a Muslim I really need to think: *Why Jesus and Mahdi, why not Moses and Mahdi or Abraham and Mahdi or Jacob and Mahdi?* This is very important for me, I have to understand!

Does not this show that this is a sign of the communities of Jesus (a) and Mahdi (a) coming together? When those who love Jesus (a) and those who love Mahdi (a)- they see these two in maximum unity with each other, so they would also be united. Especially since I have an understanding from the Qur'an that those who believe in Jesus (a) will remain until the end of the world, and we believe Muslims are also believers in Jesus (a), but Muslims and Christians always remaining in this world is very powerful. This is clearly mentioned in the Quran. God said to Jesus (a), "I'm going to raise you and I'm going to make the people who follow you above the people who deny you until the Day of Judgment."[6]

> *When God said, "O Jesus, I shall take you [r soul], and I shall raise you up toward Myself, and I shall clear you of [the calumnies of] the faithless, and I shall set those who follow you above the faithless until the Day of Resurrection.* (The Qur'an, 3:55)

Thus Jesus (a) and Mahdi (a) come together. Christians and Muslims who believe in them will come together. Of course it is not that every Muslim will believe in Mahdi (a) and it is not that every Christian will believe in Jesus (a) when he comes. I am sure many Christians will reject Jesus (a) because they will say "This is not what we expected," and many Muslims will reject Mahdi (a), as has happened with every savior; people waited for him but when they came, many of those people who were waiting denied. Like the Jews, they did not believe in Jesus (a). Anyway, there will be sincere people who follow them and they will be united.

When we have such an image about the future, there are two ways to react. One is to keep that image in your mind as a

---

[6] The Arabic text is as follows:

إِذْ قَالَ اللّهُ يَاعِيسَىٰ إِنِّي مُتَوَفِّيكَ وَ رَافِعُكَ إِلَىَّ وَ مُطَهِّرُكَ مِنَ الَّذِينَ
كَفَرُواْ وَ جَاعِلُ الَّذِينَ اتَّبَعُوكَ فَوْقَ الَّذِينَ كَفَرُواْ إِلَىٰ يَوْمِ الْقِيَمَةِ

dream and pray that it will happen. The other is that you pray but you take it as a guideline, you say I have to move towards that direction. Why is it that Mahdi (a) and Jesus (a) have not come today? If they are going to bring people together miraculously, there would be no need to wait. This means that they need some preparation, and God is not to force this plan. What would be the point in creating all human beings with free will and then at the end God takes away free will to force His plan?

God is waiting for us to understand His plan and to try to implement that plan. Unfortunately we either do not understand the plan or we just pray and do nothing. So I have taken this as my mission: that I should do my best to bring unity not only to my community but to Muslims and Christians. I think this is our historic responsibility. And this is something that the future of humanity depends on.

If we see that our Focolare friends have managed to live this unity and I see these characteristics in them, then first I should be grateful to God that there is such an experience, and secondly, I should support it. Last year in Mariapolis, I said that as a Shiʻa cleric I have no hesitation to say that I support the Focolare. For me, this is a test of my honesty, a test of my humbleness, a test of my real love for God. If I am able to see good things in people who are not from the Shia community or Muslim community, then this shows how ready I am for unity.

Of course, for me it was not difficult to say this because I do not look at the Focolare as "others." You start this with trying to see good things in others but then in the process there is no otherness. So I think the Focolare are mine and I am theirs, if they like it. So this is something that we need to establish.

I think in Islam and maybe you can also present the Christian perspective, what we have had was mostly personal and individual spirituality. We can quickly list hundreds of Muslim mystics in our minds, spiritual masters who when I compare myself to them I really feel embarrassed and sometimes I lose hope, I think who am I and who were they? So I have great respect for them. But it seems to me that most of them were not able to make their spirituality a spirituality that can motivate people to organize themselves and develop a movement or develop a spiritual organization that fulfils that requirement of being like one body.

As a person, to be spiritual is difficult, but it's much more manageable than when you want to run an organization for spirituality. It's very difficult. To run a business like Coca-Cola, Apple, or Microsoft is possible, because at the end of the day everything is based on profit and making money, etc. But to make a movement that functions internationally and efficiently, while at the same time is spiritual and over years doesn't give up its ideas- it's very important. That's why I said here – if you remember when we came to this same hall

97

– that one of the beauties of the wisdom of Chiara was that she was able to bring her ideas to the ground. There are many people who have beautiful ideas but they remain in Heaven. To bring many heavenly ideas to Earth, this is *hikmah* (wisdom), this is *sophia*. And Chiara had this idea. She didn't keep the idea in her mind or just among a few friends or in a book.

What I very much want to learn – and I suggested this idea of *Wings of Unity* to Piero and he welcomed the idea – is to see how we can spread this spirituality in a way that it forms communities, it forms movements; it forms lakes of unity, not just drops who love unity and ready to die for unity.

We don't have a problem in theology, we don't have a problem in our spirituality, but it seems that we don't have that *sophia*, that *hikmah* to understand how to bring that unity to the ground. At least I think I don't have it, maybe you think you have it. I think our generation has still not been given that wisdom to understand how we should move on to that way, but the Focolare is a very good contemporary example. We also have some examples in our history, but you can see that we still have a long distance ahead of us to go from the lake to the ocean.

There are other paradigms that we can find in Islamic sources about unity other than a body. For example, one paradigm is the paradigm of construction. In the Quran God says that the believers should be like a very firmly-built building[7]. Or our Prophet (s) said the believers are like a construction, a building. Many times I say to our people in my community, "Let's reflect on what it means to be a construction." If you have one lorry of bricks and you unload them somewhere, do you call this a construction? It's not a construction. Oftentimes our population is just like bricks – like bulk bricks – there is no organization or construction.

Many years ago when I visited Canada for the first time, one of the Focolare friends- I was actually invited by the Shia but I met one of the Focolare who passed away. You might know him, Terry. I had an interview with Salt and Light TV and he asked me – because he knew that I have a connection with the UK – *What is your opinion about the increase in the number of Muslims in Europe?* I said that I don't have any particular feeling; if good Muslims are going then I'm happy, but if Muslims are just increasing it doesn't make me happy. It's not just a matter of numbers and figures and statistics. If true believers are in Europe then I'm happy, whatever they are – Muslim or not. But if Muslims just increase it doesn't necessarily make me happy.

---

7 The Qur'an, 61:4. The Arabic text is as follows:

كَأَنَّهُم بُنْيَانٌ مَّرْصُوص

For example, sometimes I go to a town, like a town in Canada, and they say, "Thanks to God we have 14 Shia centres here." I say, "I don't know, should I be happy that we have 14 centres or does this means that they were not able to get together so they just split?" We need to have construction. If there is construction, then the growth of that construction is good. But if you just have lorries of bricks – one lorry or 10 lories or 100 lories – what can we do with this? They might even cause trouble for us.

A bulk community is not a community. Community by definition has to be organized, has to be like one body, like one building. So you need to have strong bricks first. This is the way I have defined my position in London. I say to people in London that my responsibility is this: first, as much as I can, I should make these bricks which are the members of the community strong, because if these bricks are loose, when you build on them they will collapse. With education and formation we have to make these bricks strong. But we should tell them in their formation and education that you are not just going to be a brick and enjoy your freedom; you're going to be placed in a construction. You may be used in the guest room, you may be used in the kitchen, the washroom – it doesn't make a difference. What is important is that in the end this is the only way for us to have a palace.

I was amazed with the Focolare friends. For example when they are told to go from the UK to Brazil, from UK to Istanbul, from Italy to another place- I don't think it matters to them that much. The main thing is *I am a brick of a palace; I am a member of a community, I am more than happy to do whatever suits my community the best.* But this is not the way for many of us because many of us enjoy that freedom and independence of being a brick with everything free around me. I don't want to be put in a fixed position.

So I say that my responsibility is to a) make those bricks strong through education and formation, b) make those bricks into a design – bringing organization to the community – and then c) invite other people to look at this building, by reaching out. So we have to work on three areas.

But every step is a big, big headache. How to educate- thanks to God there are many people who are interested but not everyone is interested. But more difficult than education is organizing. It's very, very difficult. Everyone – or most people – have their own personal plans for their life. The maximum they can give to God is to pray, fast, give charity, etc. But they are not ready to give their freedom of choice. I think this is the most precious thing, even more difficult than giving your life: to give your freedom of choice to the community to decide collectively what you should do for God. God is not going to ask me directly what should I do for Him. I think God speaks to us through a community of the faithful. But am I ready to listen to the community? That's the thing. So to bring organization is very, very difficult.

What I have been thinking is that I should not dream of uniting the whole Muslim community or even the Shia community, but maybe what I can dream of is to have a network. Say for example if we have 150 million Shia in the world, more or less, I don't think I am *that* capable and *that* strong that I can unite 150 million Shia. But maybe we can have a network of like-minded people who are all over the world but function as one body. They are bricks of the same construction. Then this would be a way forward. Because I don't think for the plan of Jesus (a) and Imam Mahdi (a) that we need all people to get united from the very beginning, but we need to have a sizeable number of united people who prepare. So now I am engaged in a lot of thought. How can I understand what God wants from me? How can I support people who work for unity like the Focolare? How can I bring Muslims and Christians together? How I can bring Sunni and Shia together? How can I bring Shia together? So all of these challenges are in my mind.

Therefore, I came here with humbleness and with openness to learn what the best thing would be for me to do in the next few steps. I don't expect to know everything that I have to do until I die, but at least to know the next few steps, because the most important thing is that your next step is done properly and wisely. Otherwise you can lose lots of opportunities. But if the first step is done wisely then it can create more opportunities. Thank you very much.